PARADISE STREET

Constance Congdon

BROADWAY PLAY PUBLISHING INC
New York
www.broadwayplaypub.com
info@broadwayplaypub.com

First edition: February 2018
I S B N: 978-0-88145-711-7

Book design: Marie Donovan
Page make-up: Adobe InDesign
Typeface: Palatino

PARADISE STREET was originally workshopped at the New York Theatre Workshop Vassar retreat. Subsequently, it had a reading at N Y T W. A later draft was read at The New Harmony Project. The play received a fully-staged reading at the Just Add Water Festival at Portland Center Stage, Portland, Oregon. It then received a full production at Amherst College.

PARADISE STREET made its professional debut on 20 January 2010, produced by Title Nine Theater/Title3 Company at the Attic Theater in Los Angeles. The cast and creative contriburors were:

JANE .... Molly Leland
TJ .... Lane Allison
MOTHER, WILMA, POLICEWOMAN,
    LYDIA, DOROTHY .... Danielle Kennedy
JO-JO, AMINDA, BUS DRIVER .... Jiehae Park
HITCHHIKER, COLLEGE SECRETARY,
    MAVIS, MEGA MART CORP EXEC,
    WOMAN 2 .... Jane Montosi
NURSE ANDREA, CHAI, TAMMY,
    MARTA, MIMI, WOMAN 1 .... Lorene Chesley

Director .... Courtney Munch
Lighting designer .... Christopher Singleton
Costume designer .... Rachel Weir
Sound designer .... Ryan Shields
Stage manager .... Erin Gioia Albrecht
Production manager .... Emily Rebecca Norman

CHARACTERS & SETTING

(All female)

JANE
TJ
MOTHER
SUSAN B
WILMA
POLICEWOMAN,
CHAI
ANDREA
MAVIS
LYDIA
COLLEGE SECRETARY
NURSE
MARTA
JOJO
MIMI MANNING
AMINDA

The play can be done with 7-8 actors.

Place: Five-College Area in Western Massachusetts
Time: Now

To Colleen Werthmann who invoked the charcter of TJ,
Carla Diaz who perfectly embodied her,
and to Michael Birtwistle,
who always believed in this play and gave me the most
beautiful production I could imagine.

ACT ONE

Scene One

(Rainstorm outside. TJ enters the hallway of a classic New England colonial house. A wingback chair and a beautiful little table next to it sitting on an expensive Persian rug are surrounded by stacks of boxes, some of which are partially opened—a few knick-knacks have been unpacked and one, in particular, is prominent—it's a replica of one of those fat lady Venus figures from Malta. TJ is dressed like a male trucker but with no hat and is very wet. Next to her is JANE, *dressed well, very expensive and chic under a stylish raincoat.* JANE *xs off and down a hall—we hear her knock on a door)*

JANE: *(Offstage)* Mother? Someone needs to use the bathroom.
(No answer)
Mother?
(She re-enters)
My mother's in there. She'll be right out.

(The phone rings.)

JANE: Sorry.
(She exits to answer the phone.)

(Lights up on JANE, *in another area, on the phone)*

JANE: Jane Cavett.

Liz, I've been meaning to call you. I know my
manuscript is late. But Mother and I just moved in,
barely.

(TJ *listens, and looks around at the apartment.*)

JANE: Well. it was a last-minute hire!! And, get this,
they gave me a faculty apartment!! And I have a couple
of students—haven't met them yet. And otherwise, all I
need to do is to be available for the random question—

(TJ *looks around into the hallway toward the bathroom. But
the door is still closed, so she just stands there, wet.*)

JANE: Oh, anything from what the Mayans ate or the
hegemonical assumptions of the peasant-controlled
patriarchy as opposed to the pagan-phobic, Euro-
centric church in 16th-Century Spain.

(TJ *starts to examine her surroundings. She's never seen
anything quite this expensive.*)

JANE: And no one's darkened my door—no curiosity,
I guess. Anyway, this apartment's not only great—
it's cheap. Good thing. Now that I've got Mother, no
dinero. So I leased a car! A hybrid! Well, it's a Lexus,
but it's the most fuel-efficient model.

(TJ *crosses into the living room, goes to the chair-side table,
opens the little drawer and looks inside, finds a little trinket,
pockets it.*)

JANE: Yes, Liz. I know I'm babbling, but this
manuscript will be worth the wait. Trust me.
Look, I know Marxist feminist theory was my
"brand." But I *had* to make a change. I mean, no one is
interested. That's why I switched back to the Mayans
and, well, grants were available for pre-Columbian
research and not for essays on Neolithic Maltese Venus
figures and their implied hegemony or anything
about female identity as seen through the lens of
capitalistic—

(TJ *goes to the boxes and looks inside, for something else to steal*)

JANE: I know I had a following! I know that! *The Hegemony Journal.* "Heg-emony Crick-ets" —they called themselves that, but what they were was just a small group of nerdy feminazis and all I got from that were lots of obsessive e-mails. They didn't even know what I looked like! But I was their goddess. Well, show me the money!

(TJ *spots the Maltese Venus figure. She picks it up and likes the weight of it*)

JANE: I have the media disc in my purse—

(TJ *puts the Venus figure back and freezes where she's standing.*)

(JANE *pokes her head back in and speaks to* TJ)

JANE: I'd appreciate it if you stayed in the hallway. You know, the rug. And absolutely no smoking.

(JANE *disappears again to continue her phone call. TJ returns to the "hall" and waits*)

JANE: What I have to offer—stay with me on this, Liz—is a text that hasn't gone through the patriarchical sieve, indeed, mill of hetero male interpretation. Most books are lousy with the male gaze, you know? "Gaze" —the male gaze—nothing to do with homosexual— G-A-Z-E. Right.
Look, I have someone here.
You're kidding. It's a *woman*. She needed a RIDE. I'm going to give her my plastic raincoat—that disposable one I got on the Great Goddess cruise of the Greek Isles. Now there's another book someday.

(TJ *can't resist—she dashes to the Maltese Venus figure and pockets it, returns to hallway*)

JANE: I know. I'm Mother Theresa and Fredericka Stark.
Oh, that's right. They're both dead.
Good night.
I'm exhausted. Driving in the rain is exhausting.

TJ: Real nice car.

(JANE *hangs up the phone, re-emerges, speaks to* TJ)

JANE: Say, I know what I can do, I'll give you a raincoat. I have an extra one—There.
You can keep it.

TJ: Yeah.

JANE: Well, there you go.

(TJ *says nothing.*)

JANE: You can really keep dry now.

(TJ *says nothing.*)

JANE: Aren't you going to put it on?

TJ: Sure.
(*She puts on the raincoat.*)

JANE: There. It fits.
It looks good on you.
You could wear the bag as a hat.

(*Long beat as no one moves*)

JANE: So. If you walk out the front door and turn left and go to the end of the block—it's a long block—but, anyway, that road that's going East and West is 10 and you get right on that and stick out your thumb and someone will pick you up, as I did.

(TJ *is silent.*)

JANE: So, I know you want to get going.

(TJ *is silent.*)

JANE: Well, here. Let me take you out on the front stoop and show you—

(TJ *doesn't move.*)

JANE: I think you want me to drive you.

(JANE *calls to her* MOTHER)

JANE: Mother??
Mother??
(*To* TJ)
Shall I drive you?

TJ: Where?

JANE: Where you need to go.

TJ: You don't want to go there.

JANE: Look, ever since you got in the car, I felt—. I mean, if you're in trouble, there are several women's counseling services I could—

TJ: No.

JANE: But, there are people who want to help, and—

TJ: I want your car.

JANE: Okay, I'll just get the keys…

TJ: Give me the keys.

JANE: No, I have to be the driver—the insurance, you know.

TJ: The keys?

JANE: I don't understand.

TJ: I want your car.

JANE: I said I'll drive you—

TJ: I don't want you. I want your car.

JANE: But, but you can't have my car. It's mine.

(TJ *Says nothing.*)

JANE: Look, I'm not going to give you the keys to my car.

(TJ *is silent*)

JANE: That's absurd. What you want is absurd.

TJ: Is…what?

JANE: Absurd.

TJ: Thanks.

JANE: For what?

TJ: The word.

JANE: Absurd?

TJ: Use it again.

JANE: Life is—absurd sometimes.

TJ: That's not how you used it before.

JANE: What.

TJ: Not "life." "What I want" is absurd. That's what you said.

JANE: Well…yes.

TJ: Why? Why is what I want "absurd"?

JANE: Because you want—you said you wanted…my car.

TJ: That's right. Give me the keys.

JANE: Look, you get out of here right now!

TJ: I need counseling.

JANE: Yes, you do! You certainly do! I mean, really. You do.

TJ: Give me the name of someone, some counselor, and I'll drive there.

JANE: I'll drive you.

(*Suddenly and efficiently,* TJ *coldcocks* JANE *on the head with the Maltese Venus sculpture she just picked up.* JANE *falls behind the chair and is still.* TJ *looks closely at* JANE, *then kicks her violently.* TJ *finds* JANE's *purse and car keys and exits. After a beat,* MOTHER *enters, walking with a cane. She is concentrating on her walking and doesn't notice anything, in fact, she calls for her daughter in the direction of the kitchen*)

MOTHER: Jane! Janie!! It's time for the news.
(*She lowers herself into the chair, opens the drawer to the little table, finds the T V remote and clicks on the T V, sits back to enjoy herself*)
Let's see what's happening in the world.

(*Blackout. Sound of sirens. Silence*)

Scene Two

(TJ *is traveling in* JANE's *car. She flings the Venus figure out the window. She is pushing buttons on the radio, trying to get something she likes*)

TJ: What's this?
Shit.
What's this?
Shit.
What's this?
NOTHING BUT CRAP!!

(*Then a public radio station—some classical music*)

TJ: What in the fuck is THAT?
How do you change the stations on this—
My hand hurts!!
MY HAND HURRRTTSSSS!!!!!!! FUCK YOU, RADIO!!!
FUCK YOU!!!!!
Oh, speed limit, speed limit, speed limit. Cool.
Coooooool.

(She gets the radio tuned between two stations, so that all you hear is static. This pleases her. She turns it up)

Oh YEAH, BABY!!!!!!!!!!!!! WOOOOOOOH!!!!!!

(She hits the gas and speeds up)

(End of scene)

Scene Three

(A POLICEWOMAN is interviewing MOTHER. The chair has been moved and MOTHER is sitting in it, staring straight ahead. She holds the phone in her hand. JANE's body has been removed. There is a blood stain on the floor.)

POLICEWOMAN: Does your daughter have any enemies? Has she been acting strange lately?

(MOTHER doesn't reply.)

POLICEWOMAN: I know it's painful, Mrs Cavett, but we do need something to go on.

(MOTHER doesn't reply.)

POLICEWOMAN: Anything would be helpful, any—

MOTHER: That stain on the floor.

POLICEWOMAN: Yes?

MOTHER: Someone should do something. Is someone going to do something? Blood…is very, very bad. It seeps into the wood.

POLICEWOMAN: Do you have anyone to stay with you?

MOTHER: *(She can't hear.)* Soda water. I'd do it but I have trouble bending over.

POLICEWOMAN: DO YOU HAVE ANYONE TO STAY WITH YOU?

MOTHER: "1"—is for fire. I pushed "1", didn't I?

POLICEWOMAN: Yes, you did the right thing.

MOTHER: We don't know anyone here. We're new to the area. We haven't even had a visit from the Welcome Wagon. Do they do that anymore?

POLICEWOMAN: I don't know. IF YOU COULD HELP US—

MOTHER: What do you want me to do?

POLICEWOMAN: WHAT HAPPENED TO YOUR DAUGHTER?

MOTHER: She can't help you she's gone.

POLICEWOMAN: TELL US WHAT HAPPENED TO YOUR DAUGHTER.

MOTHER: Why are you yelling at me?

POLICEWOMAN: I'm sorry.

MOTHER: What?

POLICEWOMAN: I'M YELLING SO YOU CAN HEAR ME.

MOTHER: You sound angry. And I've done nothing wrong. Besides, you are a public servant and I pay your salary through taxes which I, or my daughter Jane pays them, really, by working very hard. She was in this place below Mexico and had to be outside and a real bug got in her typewriter computer, so she couldn't press the 'm' button. Do you know how hard it is to write something about a place below Mexico without the "m" button?

POLICEWOMAN: WHAT HAPPENED HERE?! I'M NOT ANGRY.

MOTHER: Two men came.

POLICEWOMAN: *(Writing)* YES.

MOTHER: In that door.

POLICEWOMAN: DID SHE KNOW THEM?

MOTHER: No time to find out.

POLICEWOMAN: SO HOW DID THEY GET IN?

MOTHER: They just walked in—just burst in.
It was awful.

POLICEWOMAN: You're doing well. Good. KEEP
GOING.

MOTHER: They treated her badly. One of them hit her
on the breasts. Indignities—his mouth on her.

I told them to stop!!

POLICEWOMAN: DID YOU GET A GOOD LOOK AT
THEM?

MOTHER: Oh yes. I was sitting right here.

POLICEWOMAN: DESCRIBE THEM.

MOTHER: Black shoes and suitcases. Short hair.

POLICEWOMAN: WHAT WERE THEY WEARING?

MOTHER: Trousers and shirts. No ties.

POLICEWOMAN: Were—WERE THE MEN WHITE OR
BLACK?

MOTHER: I think it's impolite to mention one's race,
don't you?

POLICEWOMAN: NO.

MOTHER: They were both Negroes. With patches on
their shirts.

POLICEWOMAN: Patches? PATCHES ON THEIR
SHIRTS?

(MOTHER *points to the* POLICEWOMAN'*s uniform*)

MOTHER: Like that. With writing on them.

(POLICEWOMAN *realizes that* MOTHER *didn't see anyone
and has mistaken the paramedics for the perpetrators*)

MOTHER: One of them PUT HIS MOUTH RIGHT ON
MY DAUGHTER's!!

POLICEWOMAN: Yes, well. Well find someone to take
care of you tonight—just as long as it's not me that's all
I ask, baby Jesus.
(She exits.)

MOTHER: And then there were lots of lights. And
then you burst in, too. What's happening? WHAT's
HAPPENING? WHAT's HAPPENING?
*(She gets up and tries to destroy the television with her
cane.)*
THE STORIES FROM THE TELEVISION HAVE
LEAKED OUT INTO MY HOUSE!!!

*(POLICEWOMAN re-enter and grabs cane away from
MOTHER and manages to get hit a few times before she can
restrain MOTHER.)*

MOTHER: Jane? Janie? Where are you?
(To POLICEWOMAN)
Where did you say my daughter went?

(POLICEWOMAN just looks at her)

(End of scene)

Scene Four

*(JANE enters in a prom dress, wearing her hospital
wristband.)*

JANE: I'm in the fucking dress, Mother. Okay? And it's
just as horrible as I knew it would be. Who invented
the wrist corsage? The same white male—let's hope
he's dead—who invented high heels. And all the
underwear you have to wear under these. I forgot to
put on my panties.

*(JANE bends down quickly to check—it's true—not panties.
Sound of faint music.)*

JANE: I love this song. it's Journey…
(*Sings*)
… and drifted apart,
And here you are by my side.
And I come to you with open arms…
…He sounds like a girl almost. What's the politics of
that? Oh, I love this song. This wrist corsage has got to
go—
(*She stops abruptly because she sees the hospital bracelet on
her wrist.*)
Huh.
(*She exits.*)

Scene Five

(MOTHER *with the* POLICEWOMAN, *outside a hospital*)

MOTHER: This hearing aid makes everything sound the
same. And it's not the same. I know that. People think
you're stupid when you're old. I don't know where I
am.

POLICEWOMAN: You're outside the hospital.

MOTHER: I don't want to go in!

POLICEWOMAN: You made that clear, Mrs Cavett.

MOTHER: I don't want to go back in there. Too much
noise.

(POLICEWOMAN *lights up a cigarette.*)

MOTHER: I know that those men that broke in were
some of you.

POLICEWOMAN: They were the paramedics, yes.

MOTHER: (*About the cigarette smoking*) I used to do that.
I resigned

POLICEWOMAN: You mean you quit.

MOTHER: You have all the answers.

(POLICEWOMAN *looks at her watch*)

MOTHER: I'd like to go home. No one will come to get
me. I don't have any friends here. None of my friends
are left. My daughter doesn't have friends. She works.
That's what she does. What should I do? I can't go back
with that stain...on the floor.
My child was being...harmed and I was in the
bathroom. Without my hearing aid. I was useless.
"Someone needs the bathroom," is what I think she
said—Jane. Who was there that needed the bathroom?
I didn't know. What good is it to raise them to grow up
if you can't protect them after all those years? My life is
wasted. Will she live? Will she have scars? On her face?
Raising a girl is so different. They need to be perfect.
They can't have any scars.
Is she in there?

POLICEWOMAN: Yes.

MOTHER: Can she be...seen?

POLICEWOMAN: I don't know yet.

MOTHER: Good bye. (*She takes her hearing aid out of her
ear*)

POLICEWOMAN: THAT WON'T HELP, MRS CAVETT.

MOTHER: I CAN'T STAND ANY MORE YELLING.
And I can't go in there. I can't go in that building and
see her hurt. Do me a favor? You're a nice woman—
Kill me. I won't tell. Make it look like a suicide. You
must know a way to do that. Please. She takes care of
me. I can't live by myself anymore. I had to leave my
retirement house. I don't understand how to pay bills.
I don't understand anything. Please. Just take your
gun—

(MOTHER *grabs for the pistol in the holster and*
POLICEWOMAN *has to deal with her roughly to get her to*
stop.)

POLICEWOMAN: No. Stop it. Stop it! Mrs Cavett!!! Stop
it!!

MOTHER: Help me. Help me!

(MOTHER *dives for the gun again and almost gets it this*
time. POLICEWOMAN *pushes her down onto a bench and*
handcuffs her.)

MOTHER: What am I going to do?

POLICEWOMAN: You're going to pull yourself together
you spoiled old white woman. I am sick of you.

MOTHER: I can't hear you. I told you, I can't hear you.

POLICEWOMAN: I'm counting on that.Give me that
hearing aid.

(POLICEWOMAN *searches* MOTHER *for the hearing aid, finds*
it, then tries to put it into MOTHER'*s ear*)

MOTHER: Ow!! You're hurting me! Either kill me or
leave me alone!

(POLICEWOMAN *exits with* MOTHER)

(*End of scene*)

Scene Six

(TJ *is driving in* JANE'*s car. A young female hitchhiker,*
SUSAN *is in the passenger's seat. She is dressed in some*
Carhart gear.)

SUSAN: Awesome car.

TJ: Uh-huh.

SUSAN: Lexus, RX. Hybrid.

TJ: Put your money right here in my purse. This taxi ain't free.

SUSAN: I really like your purse. Is it Japanese? It's nice.

TJ: You don't think I could have a nice purse? Huh? 'Cause I do!

(In the purse, SUSAN finds the media disc with JANE's manuscript on it)

SUSAN: Hey, let's listen to your C D.

TJ: What the fuck are you doing?? Look, you little cunt—you put things INTO my purse. You don't ever take anything OUT!.

SUSAN: Woa. Lighten up on the offensive language.

TJ: The WHAT??? Are you saying I don't speak good???

SUSAN: N-no.

TJ: YOU *ARE* SAYING I DON'T SPEAK GOOD??!!

SUSAN: N-no. I appreciate the ride. Sorry

TJ: You think you're so great in your little outfit. You are wearing work clothes. You do any work?

SUSAN: It's just fashion, sort of. I don't care that much about costume, actually.

TJ: "Costume." You in a fucking movie or something?

SUSAN: I feel that we have gotten off on the wrong foot. I would like to apologize for everything I've said thus far.

TJ: Does that include, "I appreciate the ride sorry"?

SUSAN: N-no.

(Beat)

TJ: Well, what shall we talk about now? We're getting along so good.

SUSAN: D-did you have a bad day or something?

(TJ *laughs a lot at this.*)

TJ: You're so happy. You're so sure of yourself, walking along in the dark, fucking la-de-dah. Well, put this into your happy, la-la head. You are a pigeon. You are like deer meat in December. There are just too damn many young girls in the world and those numbers need to be less. All the drivers out there who picked up young girls, killed them and dumped their bodies and no one ever found out and these "drivers" live their lives and no one ever knows? They have pets. They fuck their wives They have some kids. They even have lawns and shit that they take care of. They even go to fucking church. Except they have this dark secret they take to their graves. And the girls? One more face on a milk carton. One more stray shoe by the side of the road. One more shallow grave in the woods.

SUSAN: You know, let me out here.

TJ: Scared you?

SUSAN: No. I just decided to go somewhere else.

TJ: Why?

SUSAN: That's why I'm hitching, so I can do what I want.

TJ: No one gets to do what they want. If they did, the world would be gone.

SUSAN: I just want to—

TJ: Because people would kill whenever they wanted to. And that would make other people want to kill and then the world would be gone.

SUSAN: Look—I just changed my mind and want to go to some friends that live near here and hang out.

TJ: Where do they live? We could both go there. I'd like to meet some new people.
I'm pretty tired of all the old ones.

SUSAN: I—I—they might not be home…

TJ: Okay.
How about up there?

SUSAN: Good.

TJ: It's the middle of nowhere.

SUSAN: That's okay.

TJ: Okay. Jump out.

(TJ *stops the car.* SUSAN *starts to get out.* TJ *guns it and they take off again.* SUSAN *screams.)*

TJ: No screaming or I will fucking kill you.

SUSAN: I hurt my hand!! In the car door! It really hurts!! *(Beat)* Maybe we can be friends.

TJ: Eat shit. YOU THINK THIS IS A FUCKING SITUATION COMEDY?!!!

SUSAN: Watch that truck!

TJ: Why?

(TJ *swerves and laughs. Sound of car horns)*

SUSAN: Help me, Jesus.

(End of scene)

Scene Seven

(In the hospital. A darkened room, except for a blue light in the area of JANE's *bed. Sounds of heart monitor, etc.—vital signs. She is there but not seen.)*

MOTHER: *(Offstage)* Jane! Janie! Where are you? Come and get me out of here. Janie. *(To whomever can hear her)* I am Mrs Foster Cavett and I don't belong here.

Someone dumped me in this wheel chair! The police in this town are incompetent!!

NURSE: *(Offstage)* Mrs Cavett! Please be quiet! Do you want to see your daughter or not? If you do, you need to be quiet.

MOTHER: *(Offstage)* I am the sick one. You clearly do NOT understand that. I'm the one who needs help.

NURSE: *(Rolling MOTHER into the room in a wheelchair)* Oh, I can see that. But right now you're here to see her.

MOTHER: But I don't see her.

NURSE: She right there, in the bed.

MOTHER: All I see are machines! I want to talk to somebody! I want to talk tan administrator.

NURSE: Mrs Cavett, your daughter is going to need you.

MOTHER: I can't hear you.

(NURSE exits.)

JANE: *(from the dark)* Ma—

MOTHER: Janie? It's Mother. Janie? It's Mama.

(JANE moans in pain)

MOTHER: Nurse? Nurse!! NURSE!!

NURSE: *(Entering)* What is it?

MOTHER: Get me out of here. I'm bothering her.

(End of scene)

Scene Eight

(TJ and SUSAN next to a drive-up A T M, but with the passenger's side next to the machine. TJ has a tire iron and has it in SUSAN's ribs. She applies pressure and SUSAN does what she's been told to do.)

SUSAN: I can't get it to work.

TJ: Bullshit.

SUSAN: No, really. I think there's something wrong with my numbers.

TJ: There's nothing wrong with your numbers.

SUSAN: Oh, wait! I just remembered! I have a new account and but the numbers, the new numbers I haven't memorized them yet.

TJ: That's supposed to be your lie? It's sad. You're pathetic. Now get some fucking money out of that machine!! And if it's less than a thousand dollars, I will use this on you. I'll beat your fucking brains out.

SUSAN: I'm not going to do it. I'll just sit here and somebody will come long and they'll see—

TJ: What?

SUSAN: This situation.

TJ: What they'll see is me beating you bloody with this sissified Lexus tire iron but it's still hard enough to make a bloody mess out of your face.

SUSAN: But they'll recognize you and send you to prison.

TJ: No, they won't. You know *why*? Because I'm invisible. If you saw me in some parking lot, you wouldn't even look at me. And if you looked at me, you wouldn't see me, You know why? 'Cause people like me, we all look alike. Poor white trash. There are the fat ones and the skinny ones. Period.

SUSAN: People like you? I don't think there's anyone like you.

TJ: You hope. NOW GET ME SOME MONEY OR I'LL SMASH YOUR TEETH OUT WITH THIS THING! GO!

(SUSAN *relents and put in her numbers. There's a hum and whir and* SUSAN *takes the money from the machine.* SUSAN *hands* TJ *a stack of 20s)*

TJ: You count them.

(SUSAN *begins counting the 20s quickly)*

Out loud!!

SUSAN: 20-40-60-80-100—my hand hurts.

TJ: Give me the money.

SUSAN: 20-40-60-80-100. 20-40-60-80-100. 20-40-60-80-100

(*Beat.* TJ *waits)*

TJ: That's all?

SUSAN: My account—I can't take more than $400 a day.
Here—you try it.
Try it!
My password is "19-99-33."
Try it!!!

TJ: See? You're trying to run things. But it's not like that.

SUSAN: If you want more money, then just break into the A T M. The money's all in there. In that little machine. I'll help you!!

TJ: If we break in there, the alarms will sound and you'll get me arrested!! We're gonna keep driving until it's tomorrow. That dumb-shit bank won't know if the sun has come up or not—after midnight, we'll be at another A T M and we will get another four hundred dollars.

SUSAN: I don't have any more money in—

(SUSAN *sees the look on* TJ'*s face and just shuts up.* TJ *sees* SUSAN'*s fear of her.)*

TJ: Now we're getting somewhere.
(*She floors the accelerator pedal*)

(*End of scene*)

Scene Nine

(JANE *enters, wearing graduation academic regalia*)

JANE: If I can just get through this day, I'll be happy,
finally. Oh, the empty ceremonies of the patriarchy.
I'm not wearing any panties. Again. Huh. Again? It's
these robes. Medieval. Medi—Evil. Medium evil. What
is that beeping sound? So irritating. Mother. Oh god
I hope she likes her seat. If she doesn't, I'll never hear
the end of it. "Jane? Janie? Why did you put me with
all the fat sweaty people?" Oh, is it time? It's time.
(*She throws her mortar board into the air, then shifts
immediately into protecting herself from falling mortar
boards.*)
Ow! These things—OW! Hurt.
(*She exits. Re-enters and picks up her mortar board*)
What am I thinking? If I ever get an academic job, I'll
need this.
(*Exits again, and then re-enters in another place*)
I was just here.
(*Exits again. Re-enters at the first place she exited*)
This is weird. Very, very Escher.
(*She exits.*)

Scene Ten

(*The side of the road.* TJ *is wearing* JANE's *bag and holding*
SUSAN *from behind,* SUSAN's *neck in the vise of* TJ's *arm.*
SUSAN's *arms are held behind her back by* TJ's *other arm.*
They are sitting)

TJ: So what do you think the stars are, huh? / They could be anything, you know. When I was holding you back there, while you pissed?/ And helped you with your little chickenshit panties. Why you wear jeans those beat up jeans and special little tiny underpants? Anyway, I was holding you, so you didn't get yourself wet and I thought a funny, you know, thought—sort of passed through my mind—I could be a mom. I could take care of a kid. It's not disgusting—all that body stuff—when a person can't do it without you, when a person would mess themselves if you weren't there. I know you thank me for that—keeping your special panties clean. / So what do you think the stars are, huh? / ARE YOU LISTENING TO WHAT I'M SAYING HERE?

(TJ *makes* SUSAN *nod her head.*)

SUSAN: I—I—I—I—

TJ: You look like someone who goes to college.

SUSAN: No.

TJ: You could afford it. I know how much those jeans cost.

SUSAN: K-Mart.

TJ: Yeah. Like you even know where one is. Where is the nearest K-Mart? Huh? Huh? This haircut cost a bundle.

SUSAN: I did it myself.

TJ: HOW? HOW DID YOU DO THE BACK?!!

SUSAN: With a mirror.

TJ: My ass! No one can do that! Do you know why?

SUSAN: No.

TJ: Because it's backwards! Because you see backwards in a mirror! What do you think I am—STUPID??

(No answer from SUSAN*)*

TJ: You'd better talk fast.

SUSAN: Like Alice in Wonderland.

TJ: What kind of crack is that?

SUSAN: No crack. It's not a crack.

TJ: What did you mean?

SUSAN: It's a book.

TJ: What is.

SUSAN: Alice in Wonderland.

TJ: I've got you by your neck and you're talking about a BOOK?

SUSAN: Alice goes through a looking-glass and goes into a land where—

TJ: A looking glass is a mirror.

SUSAN: Right.

TJ: You trying to fuck with me? You think I don't know shit like that?

SUSAN: No. Yes? No!

TJ: I can read!!

SUSAN: I'm sure you—

TJ: Let's go. Stand up.

SUSAN: I'm weak. *(Pause)* I can't breathe.

TJ: You can talk—you can breathe. Come on.

(They stand as one unit and then TJ *gets the* SUSAN *walking like a big doll, kicking her feet from behind.)*

TJ: Walk, walk, walk, Alice. / Alice.

*(*SUSAN *stops suddenly and butts* TJ *in the groin with her ass. Then turns around and butts her head into* TJ*'s solar plexis, and runs off. This headbutt has knocks the breath out*

of TJ, making her gag. It takes her a few beats to recover and when she does, she hears the sound of the ignition of the car starting.)

TJ: Fuck me! No way!

(Sound of the car peeling off in its exit)

TJ: I should have let you wet your pants. Now what the hell am I gonna do? Huh! Huh! I'm fucking lost in the middle of fucking nowhere!!!!

(Sound of car disappearing off into the distance)

TJ: YOU LITTLE UPPER CLASS PUSSY PRICK!!!
I LOVED THAT FUCKING CAR!!

(End of scene)

Scene Eleven

(JANE enters, wearing only her hospital gown.)

JANE: Where's the class? Where's the fucking class? I can't be late for my first class. I'm the fucking teacher! But…time is a construct—lateness is a construct—school is a construct—this building is…a…construct of male architectural…there's that fucking beeping again! *(She feels what she is wearing, or not wearing and is beginning to understand)*
Oh Christ oh no.
(She exits)

Scene Twelve

(SUSAN is speaking on a cell phone.)

SUSAN: Tatyanna. Oh, I'm sorry. Candelaria. Whatever. Get my mom.
She's not?
Where is she? At the club?

I thought she was finished with that! Don't the damned
Equadorians have enough aid? Oh, sorry, Candelaria.
Of course I know that's a totally different country!
No, I never thought that—you're too tall. *To be from
Equador!*
You-are-fine-as-you-are-I-am-sorry.
Mea culpa. Yo stupido Americano!!!
American-AH. Yes, I know your language honors
gender differences in a more complete way.
I'm not being disrespectful—I'm just scared.
I've been arrested.
You need to tell her I'm at the police station in Ludlow,
Massachusetts.
Policia. Sta-ti-on-ay en Ludlow.
Lud—low.
Write it down?
SHE NEEDS TO COME AND GET ME!!!!
Estoy en prisionay!

(POLICEWOMAN *enters.*)

SUSAN: AYUDA!!

POLICEWOMAN: (*Taking her cell phone back, checks the
number* SUSAN *just dialed, notes it*) Yeaaaah. So… Back to
faculty housing on Paradise Street. These academics—
they live in their own high-falutin' world, don't they?
Students must *hate* that. Right? I mean, who lives on
Paradise Street? Who the hell does she think she is? I'M
ASKING YOU A QUESTION.

SUSAN: I don't know.

POLICEWOMAN: You don't know what?

SUSAN: Who the hell she thinks she is?

POLICEWOMAN: So you do know her.

SUSAN: No!

POLICEWOMAN: Never been to Paradise Street.

SUSAN: No!

POLICEWOMAN: Me, either. Been looking for it all my life. Until last night. So here is this woman, this *visiting scholar*—it says here—just moved in, with her crazy mother, No one knows her, so who will miss her? Right? So she might have drugs, Or money for drugs. Because you're tapped out of both and Mommy and Daddy won't—

SUSAN: I didn't do it!

POLICEWOMAN: So you didn't assault this woman— Jane Cavett. Jane Cavett is her name.

SUSAN: Yes, that's right! I mean, NO, I didn't!

POLICEWOMAN: Yes or no?

SUSAN: NO!

POLICEWOMAN: Which is it?

SUSAN: You're trying to confuse me.

POLICEWOMAN: Your confusion is not my fault.

SUSAN: Then why is it happening?

POLICEWOMAN: Because you're lying?

SUSAN: I'm *not* lying! I don't do that.

POLICEWOMAN: But you steal. Isn't stealing a form of lying?

SUSAN: I—I don't know.

POLICEWOMAN: These philosophical questions stump you? Boy, somebody's parents really wasted their money. You've never even been on Paradise Street.

SUSAN: That's right.

POLICEWOMAN: But it's across from a dorm.

SUSAN: Not MY dorm!

POLICEWOMAN: But you know which dorm. And yet you've never been on that street.

SUSAN: I live across campus.

POLICEWOMAN: That's quite a hike. Were you winded when you got there? Did you ask for a drink of water? And she let you in.

SUSAN: NO.

POLICEWOMAN: Then how did you get in?

SUSAN: I don't know!

POLICEWOMAN: Or you don't remember how you got in. Because you were stoned out of your mind. Do you remember how you stole her car?

SUSAN: I didn't. Steal. Her car.

POLICEWOMAN: *Then how is it that you were apprehended driving a stolen car registered to her?*

SUSAN: I took it from the other woman.

POLICEWOMAN: This "OTHER" woman who kidnapped you.

SUSAN: Yes.

POLICEWOMAN: So, here you are—just strolling on the *interstate* miles from your school when this "Other Woman" drives up and grabs you.

SUSAN: She didn't grab me.

POLICEWOMAN: Oh, you went willingly?

SUSAN: At first. Then she scared me and I wanted to get out but she wouldn't let me.

POLICEWOMAN: But you did get out. You told me that was when you stole the car from HER.

SUSAN: I had to pee.

POLICEWOMAN: And she let you out for that?

SUSAN: But she held me, you know, while I did it. And then I bumped her in the stomach real hard with my but and turned around and used my head.

POLICEWOMAN: That must have been a first for you. / And that's when you took the car.

SUSAN: Right.

POLICEWOMAN: You were running with your pants down.

SUSAN: No, she had helped me pull them up.

POLICEWOMAN: Oooooo. She sounds scary.

SUSAN: Look! She abducted me!!

POLICEWOMAN: Where'd you get the ignition keys?

SUSAN: She left them in the ignition. So I wouldn't steal them from her. When I was, you know, peeing.

POLICEWOMAN: Let me see your hands.

SUSAN: You gonna tell my fortune?

POLICEWOMAN: You're in some movie, aren't you? Right now. People are eating popcorn, watching you. Go down the drain. With your little life.
(*She grabs* SUSAN's *right hand roughly and examines it.*)
That hurt? Definitely a contusion developing here.

SUSAN: OW!!

POLICEWOMAN: You hit that woman. With some heavy object. And that would leave a mark on your hand. AND HERE IT IS!! This woman, the first woman, not the "Other Woman" you made up—she may die. It's circumstantial, but you are fucked. See? I told your fortune after all.

SUSAN: I'm not saying another word! **I don't have to.** Miranda! Miranda!

POLICEWOMAN: That your name and home address? *(Reads name off of the paper)* "Susan B". What's your middle name?

SUSAN: It's just the initial. Come on! I'm telling the truth? Why would I fucking l lie about my middle name??

POLICEWOMAN: Maybe you have to lie about everything. Maybe that's how you keep track. It's all lies.

SUSAN: I'm named for Susan B Anthony!!

POLICEWOMAN: This Susan. She doesn't have a middle name? What is she? Your partner in crime?

SUSAN: Susan Fucking B Fucking Anthony spent her life fucking working for equal fucking rights for women!!!

POLICEWOMAN: Never fucking heard of her!

SUSAN: She's the reason we have the vote!! She went to jail for it!!!

POLICEWOMAN: What was she in for?

SUSAN: Voting Illegally.

POLICEWOMAN: You need to keep better company!! Now listen. Your name is on the list of students enrolled in a class with Jane Cavett.

SUSAN: What? What class?

POLICEWOMAN: Something unreadable about "Hedge Anonimity in 16th Century Something—archy."

SUSAN: I enrolled in a class with some teacher they hadn't hired yet!! I've never even been to the stupid class!! I didn't even want to take it!! My advisor said I had to!! None of this is my fault!!!!

POLICEWOMAN: SO YOU TOOK THIS WOMAN OUT BECAUSE YOU DIDN'T WANT TO TAKE SOME

CLASS? OR WERE YOU JUST BORED?? AND DID
YOU NEED HER LEXUS BECAUSE YOUR BMW
WAS DIRTY?? AND THE MERCEDES WAS IN THE
SHOP??? OR DID YOU JUST NEED THE MONEY
FOR YOUR HABIT? I LOVE THIS—SO MANY
MOTIVES, WE CAN PICK ANY OF THEM!

SUSAN: I want a lawyer. Hey! I'm entitled to a lawyer!

(POLICEWOMAN *grabs* SUSAN's *arms and starts checking
for needle tracks—doesn't find any. Looks on her neck*)

POLICEWOMAN: Open your mouth.
(*She uses a little flashlight to check for needle marks in the
gums*)
Take off your shoes. And socks.
(*She exits.*)

(SUSAN *takes off her shoes and socks.*)

(POLICEWOMAN *re-enters, wearing rubber gloves. She
examines* SUSAN's *feet between the toes.*)

POLICEWOMAN: Stand up.

(SUSAN *does.*)

POLICEWOMAN: Unzip.

(SUSAN *does. And* POLICEWOMAN *uses flashlight to check
in* SUSAN's *panties, pulling them out and looking down into
them. She finds nothing.*)

POLICEWOMAN: Sit down.

(SUSAN *does that. And* POLICEWOMAN *starts probing*
SUSAN's *mouth, opening the cheeks to look for needle marks.*
SUSAN *is making noises but can't speak with the cop's
fingers in her mouth*)

POLICEWOMAN: If you bite me, you will pay for it.
(*She is done.*)
There.

SUSAN: Your hands were on my feet and in my crotch and then you put them in my mouth!!!

POLICEWOMAN: Well, gosh. I'll try to remember the next time I check you for tracks—maybe later today, when we go over your story again. You wouldn't be shooting up inside your asshole, would you?

SUSAN: I have my rights!

POLICEWOMAN: Listen, you little, perfect mall girl. You were in the woman's car. And you might as well claim you were abducted by aliens because that's how flimsy your story is.   And no truckload of fancy lawyers are gonna save your fancy little ass. Let's go.

SUSAN: Mommy!! Mommy!!

(End of scene)

Scene Thirteen

(Outside a convenience store—TJ is eating a Twinkie she just bought. She is freezing. A young woman, CHAI, comes up to her, holding a cup of coffee.)

CHAI: Excuse me.

(TJ doesn't answer)

CHAI: Excuse me.

TJ: Yeah?

CHAI: You dropped this.

(CHAI hands her a credit card. TJ takes it and pockets it. CHAI offers her the cup of coffee)

CHAI: Here. / Come on. I can see you're cold and everything.

(CHAI hands her the coffee. TJ takes it, takes off the lid, smells it.)

CHAI: I didn't drink out of it.

(TJ *can't resist and starts hungrily drinking it*)

CHAI: Are you who I think you are?

TJ: Nope.

CHAI: Are you Jane Cavett?

TJ: I'm not anybody.

CHAI: No. Everybody's somebody. You taught me that. If you are whom I think you are. 'Cause I kinda read your name. On your card.

TJ: Why you reading somebody else's credit card?

CHAI: You are so kinda combative, so male-identified. I'm not criticizing. I just didn't expect it. I read one of your essays and it changed my life. I lacked courage. I lacked cultural context, as a woman, but your essay on the de-codification of the hegemony of Western capitalist and cultural memes...wow. Just wow. *(Beat)* So I thought you'd be strong, yeah, but still, you know, fem.

TJ: What kind of crap is that?

CHAI: Oh! Oh man, I didn't mean—I didn't mean to—

TJ: Than why'd you do it, if you didn't mean to?

CHAI: There's Jane Cavett. That honesty. / I just wanted to...talk to you.
(Hands her a candy bar)
Here. Have my Mounds.

TJ: *(Unwraps it and begins to devour it)* God, I love these Mounds to death.

CHAI: I believe that we humans need to do service by helping each other and so I'm helping you and besides it's some kind of major destiny that brought us together because I read one of your essays and I thought it was brilliant. It was in this very special, small journal called "Hegemony Cricket."

TJ: You wanna buy me a sandwich? I've been walking. My fucking sister stole my car.

CHAI: That sucks.

TJ: Yeah. Break Mom's heart and everything. Wish I knew where she was. I'd like to set her straight.

CHAI: I just bought this cheese and ham thing. / Want it?

(TJ *tucks into it in a major way.*)

CHAI: God. You are so carnivalesque / I don't think it's possible that you're NOT that Jane Cavett.

TJ: Is there more than one?

CHAI: I mean, you're the writer, aren't you?

TJ: I'm whoever my credit card says I am. / I like to keep things simple like that.

CHAI: Oh, it is you, it is you. You write so eloquently about irony as a meme-maker in the language of the Other. You tell the truth about the rigidity of female identity in a capitalistic hegemony. You are really something.

TJ: Not really.

CHAI: Oh, yes you are! Oh yes, you are! Anybody who has written as cogently as you have about post-postmodern feminism is somebody, believe me. I could just stand near you all day and wait for the next quanta of eloquence to come out of your mouth.

TJ: Is there a Mickey Dee's around here?

CHAI: O-okay.

(End of scene)

Scene Fourteen

(JANE, *still in her hospital gown, enters at a dead run and is blocked by an invisible wall.*)

JANE: Where?
(She tries to exit another way, is blocked.)
Where?
(Tries another exit, is blocked)
Where?
(Running from exit to exit, blocked at every one of them)
Where? Where? Where?
WHERE??
(Suddenly, she's at the edge of a large hole. She tips forward, looks down, raises her arms to keep her balance, but it doesn't work)
I'M FALLING!!!!

(Blackout. End of scene)

Scene Fifteen

(*At* CHAI's *apartment.* LYDIA, *the roommate, is there, a sincere college intellectual, a little stoned and smoking a joint. TJ is eating whatever is available. There's trash from Mac Donald's everywhere.*)

LYDIA: CHAI and I found your essay in the Fourth Wave Wymyns' bookstore in a little journal called the Orchid? Used to be called Qwim? It was a reprint from that Hegemony Cricket cyber zine. Anyway, we think you are some kind of undiscovered genius. And here you are—like your life is a deconstructed slash reformatted collage of what it means to be a male. I mean, your costume and entire presentation of self enacts a truly performative engendering of an already embodied identity in the context of a previously established and overwhemingly heterosexual cultural matrix. And more people need to experience that. Live.

TJ: You got something to drink?

CHAI: Here's some Odwalla.

TJ: You got anything to put in it?

CHAI: Like…what?

TJ: Gin.

LYDIA: That is so cool.

TJ: Vodka? *(Takes a hit off the joint)*

CHAI: I've got a couple of miniatures of something.

(CHAI goes to get them. Returns. Hands TJ two miniatures)

CHAI: Old Grandad.

(TJ takes it, opens it and pours it into her Odwalla drink. Then takes a swig. It's not good but she's happy to have the booze)

TJ: What's the other one?

CHAI: Dickel. These were jokes—cause this one looks like a dick and Old Grandad was, you know, an old guy—

TJ: *(Taking the Dickel miniature and swigging some of it)* It's better as a chaser.

LYDIA: You probably have realized by now that I created an awful gaffe earlier by using an entirely reactionary discourse as the background by which I was trying to describe your performance of self so that any attempt I might enact at erasing, or at least destabilizing, that pre-existing metanarrative I subjected you with can only be grounded in a marginalized and abjectified decentralized subject-position, a place I can't imagine you ever inhabiting. *(Silence)* I hope you're not angry with me.

TJ: Hell, no.

LYDIA: Wow! *(Turns to* CHAI*)* Wow.

CHAI: You're not quite what we expected.

TJ: Oh yeah. Well, I'm not myself on account of feeling marginalized by your gaffe.

LYDIA: I'm so sorry.

TJ: Just don't let it happen again.

LYDIA: I won't.

TJ: Because the patriarchy is watching. And all the male gaze, too. It's lousy.

LYDIA: I knew you were a genius and I expected that kind of brilliance but I didn't expect, and I hope this isn't another gaffe, I didn't expect wisdom.

TJ: Oh, you always need to expect that kind of shit because if you don't, it might come to your doorstep and no one's home. I'm sleepy so I'm going to sleep. *(She goes to sleep.)*

CHAI: *(Trying to wake her up)* Jane? Jane? JANE!!

LYDIA: We could, like, watch her sleep.

(They sit and watch her for a beat)
Woa, she is out.

CHAI: Let's surprise her and French braid her hair.

(CHAI help put a blanket over TJ and lights down on LYDIA French braiding TJ's hair)

(End of scene)

Scene Sixteen

(SUSAN still in custody and on a payphone.)

SUSAN: Yeah, Mom.
The lawyer isn't here yet. Well, they won't let me wait.

Couldn't you hire that guy—that guy who did your divorce?

Why not? You paid him enough.

No! No, I'm not complaining. I know I'm in trouble, but it's not my fault!!

I was fucking kidnapped!!

No, I wasn't hitching!!

I'm telling you she grabbed me!!

They say I assaulted this professor and now she's in the hospital.

I DON'T KNOW THE WOMAN AND NO IT HAS NOTHING TO DO WITH MY GRADES THIS SEMESTER!!

This lady—*woman, okay WOMAN*—that she stole the car from.

Of course, I don't. I don't know anything about any of this.

The bitch who kidnapped me!!

WOMAN OKAY WOMAN W O M A N!!

Rough Trade? Where in the hell did you get a term like that?

Lesbians don't have rough trade, Mother

No, I'M NOT A LESBIAN!!

YES, I WOULD TELL YOU!!

STOP TRYING TO BE HIP AND HELP ME!!

OFFSTAGE VOICE: Ya done with the fucking phone or not??

SUSAN: Okay, I have to ask this. Are you sure a woman lawyer will be…strong enough?

Those are lawyers on television, Mother.

She needs to convince them I don't have a motive!!

What would I want with a used Lexus? I HAVE A FUCKING TRUST FUND!!!

OFFSTAGE VOICE: You got one minute!!

SUSAN: Okay. Okay. Okay. Okay. Right. It's so unjust,
Mother.
I mean, what good is it being rich if they still put you
in jail whenever they want to?

OFFSTAGE VOICE: Thirty seconds!

(*But* SUSAN *has already hung up the phone*)

SUSAN: My name is Susan B Gore-Austin and I don't
belong in this place!! I am innocent!!! I am a good girl!!!
I mean, WOMAN!! I AM A GOOD WOMAN!!!

(*GUARD comes from nowhere and, without, pausing,
sweeps* SUSAN *offstage. End of scene*)

Scene Seventeen

(*JANE enters, exhausted. She sits on stage floor and then tips
over.* NURSE *enters, speaks to her but doesn't move*)

NURSE: Come on. There you go. We're going to get
you propped up here. Fluff these pillows, get you
straightened around. That's what we need. Right?
You've been flailing around a bit, but now you're quiet.
There, there.

(*JANE sits up.*)

NURSE: Open those eyes?

(*JANE looks at the* NURSE.)

NURSE: There you are. Hi. Welcome back. Come on,
keep those eyes open.
Stay awake. You're fine, you're fine, you're fine.

(*JANE stands.*)

NURSE: There you go. Hello. You've been really sick
and we had some scares but you're doing good now. I
bet you want to know what day it is. It's Tuesday.

Jane? Stay with us. Don't close your eyes. You have
flowers here you haven't seen.

(JANE *begins the slow walk to the* NURSE.)

NURSE: There you are. Hello. Are you hungry? Doctor's
taken the trach tube out and now we have some jello.
Let me turn on the television.

(NURSE *produces a T V remote and clicks it—suddenly
there's the sound of the world flooding in—a mix of
broadcast, music, people talking, traffic, babies crying, dogs
barking, wind, rain. This stops* JANE.)

NURSE: Hey, don't doze off now. We need to keep you
awake. Come on. Join the world. It's waiting for you.
Oh! And look what's here! RED jello.

(JANE *runs to the* NURSE, *like a child to a mother.*)

NURSE: That's a girl. That's a good girl.

(NURSE *disappears.* JANE *speaks to* ANDREA, *who is sitting
next to her.*)

JANE: Marx. Hegemony. Thousands of years before
all the writing about, One, a mode of thought, and
Two, this particular word for hierarchical systems, the
Mayans thought the wheel was the symbol of death so
they refused to use it to travel with death rolling you
along, away from everything. No wheels at all and
they still invented time. And women knew it already
because they tended the dead. Women were clocks
themselves because of their menses and the moon was
round and a wheel but someone knew it wasn't flat. A
ball, some young boy played that dangerous game and
said this black ball is like the moon? Therefore. Chuck
Close painting a portrait with paintings *Close* up but far
back a face of a woman who paints the Golden Mean.
See? Flat. Not like a saddle. A riderless horse the bears
of heaven would never ride. But a rabbit—a rabbit
could be in the moon. So how did the schism come? It's

the counting, counting, counting, counting, counting,
count of down feathers as units of consciousness,
calling it time. And they kept score in the game as soon
as they had time, had death. They had all the parts of
time including number of breaths. And then life was
a collection of units. So life became a fearsome thing
because it became only a matter of Time. Then trying
to catch it, to stop it—no—and running from it and
each other. And a watch disappeared. Like that. I think
it was mine. With the woven band. And now we've
come to this: if Hopi men do the weaving, who does
the fabric of the universe? Who has it? I never saw it.
I'm the voice in my head that never shuts up. Only
it's someone else's voice. But it's running. After the
Mayans.

ANDREA: That's better, but I couldn't quite hear all
the syllables. Now watch my mouth as I say it. "My
mother lives in a house—with me."

JANE: I have complex thoughts. I have ideas. I am not
some table trying to learn to speak in forks and elbows!

ANDREA: Okay. That's better. But next time through,
try to get the "t""h" in "mother". "Th" "th"—try it—
just the "th" for me.

JANE: Use your dog ears. There's got to be some
frequency you can turn to. The Mayans left only
writing and we hear them!

ANDREA: Don't get upset. Everything is all right. Just
slow down and try one sound. Right now you're
moving your jaws too much and you might bite your
tongue.
Here.
(*She grasps* JANE's *head between her hands and then begins
to move* JANE's *jaw for her.*)
See you don't have to open your mouth that wide. I
think you're doing that out of frustration. Most of the

time we don't speak with our mouth open like that.
Watch me.
Hello, Jane. How are you today? See? My mouth
opened an inch at the most. Hello, Jane. How are you
today? Here, honey, try to say something.

JANE: *(Every effort she can muster goes into trying to
making herself heard and understood)* F u c k y o u.

ANDREA: Fantastic! You got the "F" the "K" and the
"Yuh" sounds and those are difficult. Now try the "th".

JANE: You are a stupid cunt and I can't believe you're
doing this for a living.

ANDREA: Not coming through. Try it again.

JANE: CUNT WHORE PUSSYTWAT BITCH!

ANDREA: It's all right to be angry, but I didn't get one
word of what you said. / Now let's go back to making
ourself understandable.

(End of scene)

Scene Eighteen

(At LYDIA's *and* CHAI's *apartment.* TJ *has awakened with
her hair in a French braid)*

TJ: What the fuck did you do to my hair? You fucking
fucks. Where are you, you little
pussies!

*(*LYDIA *and* CHAI *enter in their nighties, chasing* TJ *around
while holding a cheap full-length mirror like you buy at
Target. They are trying to get her to look at herself in it.
Instead,* TJ *has started to tear at the hairdo until she catches
herself in a mirror. And as soon as that happens,* TJ *becomes
transfixed.)*

TJ: Damn.

CHAI: We were overcome with this compulsion—

LYDIA: —to exercise our atavistic rituals of grooming.

CHAI: I mean, what girl—woman doesn't like a makeover?

TJ: You made me look like a fucking hooker!!!

LYDIA: Our intention was to bond much like primates in the wild.

TJ: I look like some fucking bar slut!!

CHAI: Here. Take it all down then.

LYDIA: I'll help you. Shall I help you?

TJ: Don't touch me! / Now leave me the fuck alone!!!

(CHAI *and* LYDIA *exit. Long beat, as* TJ *makes certain she's completely alone before she speak— [Softly, to her image in the mirror].)*

TJ: Who the fuck are *you?*

(End of scene)

Scene Nineteen

*(*MOTHER, *sitting in her wheelchair, is with* ANDREA *the speech therapist, who is sitting in an office furniture type chair and holding a manila folder.* JANE *sits in a chair.)*

MOTHER: What do you mean, disabled? I'm the one who's disabled.

ANDREA: I know it's a shock.

MOTHER: She woke up.

ANDREA: She had a severe head injury.

MOTHER: She's young.

ANDREA: Mrs Cavett, you daughter took a major blow to her frontal lobe. Her speech is impaired and will

probably stay that way for the rest of her life. She
has balance problems and a weakness in her left arm
from permanent nerve damage. And so there's this
dichotomy of who she was and what she has become.

MOTHER: *Whom* she has become. Not *"what"*.

ANDREA: Of course. I'm sorry, I meant "whom."

MOTHER: No, you didn't. You meant "what". As if
she's no longer human.

ANDREA: I think we've taken her as far as we can.

MOTHER: Is that another way of saying the health
insurance has run out?

ANDREA: Jane had no health insurance, Mrs Cavett.
That's why you had that talk with the hospital
administration about payment. Remember?

MOTHER: Jane does all of that. My husband used to do
all of that sort of business, then J
ane took over because she's so smart.

(MOTHER *looks at* JANE *sitting silently.*)

MOTHER: How will I manage if she's disabled? Who
will do the shopping? Who will get me my meals? Who
will drive me to the doctor? Who will buy me another
television?

ANDREA: Someone will come to the home and help
with the transition.

MOTHER: The transition? To what?

ANDREA: There may come a time, Mrs Cavett, when
you might have to go to work to be the breadwinner
for the family since your daughter is permanently
disabled.

MOTHER: But Jane's fellowship.

ANDREA: There's no money left in the fellowship.

MOTHER: I expect that if you call the college, / But…
The phone doesn't work. Janie didn't pay the bill. I told
her to. But she didn't.

ANDREA: She was in a coma.

MOTHER: She didn't want to wake up! She didn't want
to come back! You made her come back!! And I made
her come back, too. And now she's mad at me for that.
She won't talk to me.

ANDREA: She has speech problems.

MOTHER: If she wanted to talk to me, she would.
(To JANE*)* And she knows that.
(Back to ANDREA*)* You may go now. And thank you for
your time.

ANDREA: Mrs Cavett, this is my office.

MOTHER: I'm going to stay here until the world goes
back to the way it was before.

ANDREA: Look. I came in this late especially to talk to
you. And now I'm going home. Jane? Jane. Why don't
you come with me and I'll take you back to your room.

JANE: Not yet. Listen. Hundreds and hand-written,
Illustrated. Astronomical. Calculations. Stories.
History. Descriptions. And they burned it. Without
reading a word. We need to learn from history.

ANDREA: What do you want, Jane? Slow down.

JANE: Worse than Alexandria. How many teeth does a
jaguar have? It may be wrong, but it would be nice to
know, wouldn't it? Wouldn't we care to know? You
see, wait! Wait! Noooooo,

ANDREA: Jane, you're getting agitated. Don't —

JANE: Look. The sun—somebody stole the sun. Not a
myth—this really happened. And the sun rises and sets
in there because that's all it knows. It doesn't know
it's in that cave. But we have to rescue it. And there

are songs floating around in there. And poems. And stories. Lots of untold stories. And I know where it is. The sun cave, Andrea. And you have to help me, Andrea, Andrea.

ANDREA: My name! I heard my name! Good job. But the rest—

JANE: Just listen to me. Just listen. Please. Please.

ANDREA: I'll get your memo board.

MOTHER: Jane? I have to go to the bathroom.

JANE: (About ANDREA approaching with the memo board) Don't. Don't. Just listen. Listen carefully. NOOOOOOOOOOO! (She flings the memo board away.)

MOTHER: Jane? What are you doing? What is all this? This is not what we do. Now I have to go to the bathroom and I need you to take me. Jane? Janie, do you hear me!

(JANE, crosses to MOTHER and wheels her out. ANDREA follows)

(End of scene)

Scene Twenty

(SUSAN, enters dressed in prison orange, using a mop to wipe down the stage or part of it. It should seem as though the mopping that we can see her do on stage is a continuation of a big job that began offstage so when she mops herself into a corner, she is trapped. There's no way out except by walking some distance over her work.)

SUSAN: Crap!

(End of scene)

Scene Twenty-One

(JANE *enters using a walker. She lowers herself into her mother's wingback chair. Then she notices the wetness, gets herself up and turns over the seat pillow and sits back down.* COLLEGE SECRETARY, *a woman, enters.*)

COLLEGE SECRETARY: I just let myself in I hope that's okay.

JANE: O—Kay. W-wel—

(COLLEGE SECRETARY *interrupting and talking even faster—*JANE'*s speech impediment getting to her:*)

COLLEGE SECRETARY: The dean would have come but she's so busy. We're all busy.
Everyone is busy. This time of year. Any time, actually. The fellowship office sent over this to give to you..

JANE: What?

COLLEGE SECRETARY: It's a day-runner. With a calculator. It's an academic calendar. See? September to September. I get them for all the faculty so they said it would be okay—good, really—to give you one, As a good-bye gift.
(*Long beat*)
I'm on my lunch hour, actually. Some of the other secretaries and I walk at lunch instead of eat. That's why the running shoes.

JANE: Y—you nee—d to—

COLLEGE SECRETARY: Why don't you use your memo board?

(COLLEGE SECRETARY *finds a plastic write and erase memo board where* JANE *has tried to hide it.* JANE *nods vigorously in the negative.*)

COLLEGE SECRETARY: Because it's easier. For anyone who has to talk to you.

I just have to—I need to say this: I didn't agree with the way they treated you and a lot of us secretaries thought it was terrible. They could've bent the rules and let you stay in college housing until you got better. After all, you were a guest of the college and you wouldn't have been here if they hadn't invited you and so it's kinda their fault. Because you would've stayed where you were wherever that was—

JANE: Mmmm—eggs—ee—k—k-o

COLLEGE SECRETARY: Don't they have a lot of crime down there? Or maybe I just think that because Mexicans are always getting arrested trying to cross that river whatever it is. But it's so weird that you would come up here and be a victim of a crime. And in such a nice house, too. What about that chair?

(JANE *doesn't answer*).

COLLEGE SECRETARY: I'll just have physical plant take it away. Oh man, the old smelly furniture they give you in college housing. Table's nice. And the keys! Oh god, can't forget the keys. I wouldn't want to face Darth Dan without the keys. We call him that because he's so 'Oooooo" about the keys. No one ever wants to face him when they've lost keys.

(JANE *opens the little drawer in the table and gives her the keys.*)

COLLEGE SECRETARY: Where are you going?

(JANE *gets memo board and writes a big question mark on it, shows it to* COLLEGE SECRETARY.)

(Horn honk)

COLLEGE SECRETARY: Hey, your ride is here.

(JANE *exits using the walker.* COLLEGE SECRETARY *yells out the door to whomever is* JANE's *ride.*)

COLLEGE SECRETARY: She's on her way!
(She exits.)

Scene Twenty-Two

(A continuation of the scene, cross-fade to JANE, *using her walker, making her way across the stage, slowly. as* CHAI *and* LYDIA *appear. They wave.)*

CHAI: *(To* TJ *as* JANE*)* Ms Cavett? We're over here!

(But it is not to JANE, *they are waving at. It is* TJ, *hair done and looking just like* JANE *before the assault, coming towards them, carrying lots of shopping bags from upscale department stores. She drops the bags and* CHAI *and* LYDIA *run to pick them up, but are stopped by* TJ*'s entrancing new look.)*

TJ: What the fuck?!! These shoes are fucking HELL.

LYDIA: Wowww.

CHAI: Yeahhhhhh.

TJ: You mean, this is all it takes? God, this world is full of crap.

(She kicks her bags towards CHAI *and* LYDIA *and exits.* CHAI *and* LYDIA *grab the bags and run after her)*

END OF ACT ONE

ACT TWO

Scene Twenty-Two

(Months later. In the evening. With a cane, JANE *enters the downscale apartment she shares with her mother.* JANE *is dressed in a rumpled version of a woman's "power suit." She's been out looking for a job. She sits, exhausted, in a blue nylon camp chair [Linens & Things $7.25].)*

MOTHER: *(Offstage)* Jane? Jane?

JANE: Yes.

MOTHER: Jane?

JANE: Yes.

MOTHER: Janie?

*(*JANE *can't bring herself to talk any more)*

JANE: W-WHAT!? W-WHAT do you W-Want?

MOTHER: Are you home?

JANE: N-NO.

MOTHER: *(Entering)* You are, too. You're right here. Do you know where the manicure set is? When we've moved, when those huge hairy men came and moved us, everything got discombobulated and I can't find half of the things—

JANE: W-which Half?

MOTHER: Well, dear, that question doesn't make any sense. See? This is part of your problem now. You

don't make sense all the time. And it makes it difficult
for me, your mother. Because having a daughter who
doesn't make sense all the time is confusing for me and
I am easily confused. I just had a thought. At your job
interviews, do you have to speak? Maybe they won't
notice that way.
(She exits, then re-enters.)
Oh. What are we having for dinner?

(JANE doesn't respond.)

MOTHER: Oh, I see. You are tired. And dinner is too
much. I understand.
(She wanders off.)
I had something, a little snack, at six or so.
(She re-enters, then wanders off again.)
I guess I'll just lie down and wait for morning to come.
And be thankful when it does or something like that.
(She exits)
Good-night.

(JANE can't seem to stay awake. She nods off…)

Scene Twenty Four

(…and is suddenly awakened by—)

VOICEOVER: *(P A in the office)* Number eighty-one.

JANE: *(To anyone who can hear)* Eight—tee? I—have…
eighty.

VOICEOVER: Stay in line. You won't get your benefits
unless you stay in line.

JANE: I was in – line.

VOICEOVER: Number eighty-two.

JANE: I have—num-ber eigh-ty!

*(JANE crosses towards a door. A WELFARE EMPLOYEE
emerges from behind another door)*

WELFARE EMPLOYEE: Hey, hey, where do you think you're going? Wait until your number's called.

JANE: My number—

WELFARE EMPLOYEE: Look around you. There a lot worse-off people than you. You never been to the welfare office before?

(The WELFARE EMPLOYEE *disappears again behind the door.)*

VOICEOVER: Number eighty-four.

JANE: But, Eight—tee. Where Eight-tee?.

(The WELFARE EMPLOYEE *re-emerges and walks briskly past* JANE.*)*

TH—Th-they…skipped…eightee—three.

WELFARE EMPLOYEE: Is your number eighty-four?

JANE: No—

WELFARE EMPLOYEE: Then, why do you care? *(She exits)*

JANE: I – I –

VOICEOVER: Number eighty-seven
(Beat)
Number eighty.

(Just then, the stage goes black.)

MOTHER: *(from offstage)* Janie? Jane! Did you pay the electricity bill? I told you!!

(End of scene)

Scene Twenty-Three

(The Gyno-Herstorical Seminar. TJ, as Jane, sits at a dias, with a microphone in front of her. She is being introduced by MAVIS, *an expensively dressed academic in her thirties)*

MAVIS: And those are just some of the achievements of our guest, Jane Cavett. And we want to thank her chaffeur, Lydia MacDonald-Stein, a brilliant student I had the pleasure of teaching when I was at the Other School whose name we won't mention. Ms Cavett is going to present a paper on the position of women in Mayan hegemony, with a soupçon of Marxist theory, we hope...or something else. She said she didn't want to read something, but rather dialogue with all of us. And she agreed to join in our continuing discussions of gyno-future in the twenty-first. Another thank-you goes to our sponsor who supplied the funds for Ms. Cavett's visit. Thank you, Ms. Panda-Panji-Rabinowitz. Where are you, Pan? Pan? There you are! Our benefactor everyone. And her fan club, the Hegemony Crickets are here as well.

(Sound of the clicking of toy crickets. MAVIS smiles and says evenly.)

MAVIS: Stop that.
(To TJ)
And now the floor is yours, Jane.

TJ: *(Leaning into the mic)* Hey.

(Sound of toy crickets clicking an ovation. MAVIS glares. Cricket sounds peter out. Pause as they wait for her to say something.)

TJ: I'm Jane Cavett.

(Sound of one stray toy cricket)

MAVIS: Well, I'll ask the first question.What do you think, Jane, of the hegemonic problematization of gender-based issues? Isn't that just a co-opting by the patriarchy of another paradigmatic take-over, coup, if you will?

(TJ just stares at her. MAVIS smiles, waiting for an answer. TJ leans into the microphone)

TJ: I will.

(Beat. MAVIS *doesn't get it)*

MAVIS: Oh. That is it! "I will." Instead of being
Bartleby, the Scrivener, you are Jane, the willing
participant!
My will is my hegemony. Let it rule me. Because
it's mine. I am Pinocchio—Pinocchia—and my will
is my Hegemony Cricket, that meta-mythological
creature of conscience, not unlike the Sphinx, but
choosing cajolment of the master over murder through
devourment.

TJ: Right.

MAVIS: So let me ask you this, a confrontational yet
essentialist question but inspired by your essay:
"Phallocentric and Class-Ignorant Assumptions That
Rule the Engenderment of Identity Issues in Cultural
Anthropology" —In reference to the male organ: to
the extent that its absence or presence transforms
an anatomical difference into a major classification
of humans, and to the extent that, for each subject
this presence of absence is not taken for granted, is
it not reduced purely and simply to a given, but, in
fact, is the problematical result of an integra-and
intersubjective process—the subject's assumption of his
own sex?

TJ: No.

MAVIS: Would you care to elaborate?

TJ: No.

MAVIS: So, can I conclude from these almost zen-like
answers of yours, these koans which we, the audience,
pack with meaning, that you are taking a stand against
anthropological sophistries?

TJ: Yeah.

MAVIS: I see through you, Ms. Cavett. The performative nature of this event is dominated, i.e., controlled by your presentation of self, this monosyllabic creation constructed from
metanarratives that shriek out against the paradigmatic dominant, class-ignorant movement that feminism has become.

TJ: What? Now see, you're so close to saying something I think I agree with. But I don't know what the fuck you're saying.

MAVIS: Oh, oh, here we go. What the fuck I am saying. "What" —implying an already constructed hidden paradigm of identification; "the" assumption of the recognition of individuation of the next word, "Fuck"—rich with levels of implication, allusion, illusion of and to a gynocentric co-opting of the domination in the act; "am"—how can we begin to unpack this verb without deconstructing all of western history; "

TJ: You need to shut up!

MAVIS: Yes. Our own language—we need to find it and stop remaking the language of the patriarchical—

TJ: What you need. What all you rich little cunts need is a job—or two—or three because that's what it usually takes to make enough money to pay the rent and feed yourself. I'm going to tell you how to make ketchup soup, so you might want to write it down in one of those notebooks of yours. Okay—go into a Mickey Dee's and get some packets of ketchup—they just don't leave them out any more, so you need to *pretend* you're getting them for someone else, someone in a car. And then you say, "Oh—and an extra cup, so we can share the milkshake with my grandma." Do not say "drink" or they'll give you a tiny, crappy cup. You need a cup that will hold some milkshake and not collapse as "Grandma" drinks from it. Then you need hot water and don't go looking for it in some restroom because none of them run it any more. So leave the Mickey Dee's and go to a Cumby or a Circle-K or a 7-11. Walk in and go to the coffee maker place they all have, waving your cup, like "I just need to heat up my tea," or "dilute this crappy coffee I got at MacDonald's I shoulda bought your coffee." Go to the hot water spigot—it's usually part of the Bunamatic or whatever coffee maker they have—pour the hot water into your cup, while pocketing some salt and pepper packets and a stirrer and walk out saying "Thanks!" And then tuck yourself away somewhere outside because now you're going to cook. Empty all the packets of ketchup into the hot water, as many as you've been able to get, stir, and then add the salt and pepper because ketchup is way too sweet—and then enjoy it. It's free soup. And those of you with the toy cricket things whatever? Stuff them up your twats.

MAVIS: Any questions? Anybody? Anybody? Please?

(End of scene)

Scene Twenty-Four

(JANE, DOROTHY, TAMMY [all but except TJ], are onstage and wearing blue Mega Mart vests. They've been singing the MegaMart song, except for JANE. DOROTHY is leading them to tune of "My Country Tis Of Thee")

DOROTHY: Megamart is our home

(And TAMMY:)

DOROTHY & TAMMY: From which we'll never roam.
We're happy here.
Our customers are great
On the floor, we're not late
Megamart, you're the one

Best store in America.

M! E! G! A! Squiggly! M! A! R! T!

DOROTHY: Okay. First of all, the squiggly sucks. It's
supposed to be your whole body, not just your hips
because if you use your hips it looks like you're
a stripper. And Tammy, yeah, hon, Just use your
shoulders and hips to make the squiggly. You were
looking like an Indian dancer I mean from India. And
they're another religion so we can't do that or every
church in this town will come over and make us do
some, you know, Christian movement whatever that is.
Sorry, but I have to speak my mind. We're not in one of
those Moslem countries. Okay? I have to be me. I have
freedom of speech. And it's not against God or even
Allah or Jesus, god knows. I love Jesus. Who wouldn't?
And I go to church. Sometimes. So I'm not—well,
whatever—let's get back to the song.

(Looks at clock)

Oh dangit. We have to be on the floor in two minutes.
No time to pee, Let's get at our stations. Store is
opening in—four minutes.

(To JANE)

Except you, kid.

So what's up with you? You weren't singing.
Everybody's supposed to sing.

JANE: can't.

DOROTHY: Everybody can sing. You don't even have to
be on key or anything. Didn't you listen? It's not like
we're the—ah—Mormon Tabernacle Choir.

JANE: don't want to

DOROTHY: Well, who does? It's seven thirty in the
effing morning! But we all do it. Because it's our job. So
what makes you so dang special?

JANE: *(Her emotion causing her to lose her ability to separate her words)* I am one of the NOT special people. I know that.

DOROTHY: Hey, kid. Take a Midol or something. Then come back and do these returns. Big sale in the junior department over the week-end and those little girl and their mothers are such pigs. I mean, look at this—stuff. All these little items go with other little items to make some outfit.
(Picking one of the items up)
Oh, this is cute.
(Throw it back into the bin)
So either take a Midol or take these returns out on the floor and put them all where they belong.

(JANE exits in the "dressing room" area of the store, where TAMMY is. DOROTHY separates more clothes and with a vengeance)

DOROTHY: Why do I have to work with the handicapped? Can you tell me that, huh, God? This damned doo-gooder policy like that's gonna make everyone forget that everything in here is made by children in China and we're working our butts off for six dollars and fifty-cents an hour.

TAMMY: *(Offstage)* Either do something about it or shutup, Dorothy!

DOROTHY: Tell me what to do and I'll do it!

(WILMA, an older woman, enters, pushing another bin of clothes.)

WILMA: All this crap was found in housewares. Most of it is clothes. People just wander around picking up shit and dropping it when they're tired of it.

DOROTHY: Watch your language, Wilma. You know how that—

WILMA: Sorry, hon. I'll do these for you.

DOROTHY: *(Whispering about* JANE*)* Use the crip, okay?
Please. She needs to snap out of it.

WILMA: Where is she? *(Indicates offstage, where* JANE *is)*
Come on, hon. Come on out. No one's gonna hurt you.

DOROTHY: No, somebody already did. Unless she was
born that way. She's got a crease in her skull your can
see if you look real close at her hair.

*(*JANE *enters)*

WILMA: There she is…Miss America.

DOROTHY: I thought I was that. No, it's you, Wilma.
You're Miss America.

TAMMY: *(Offstage)* We all are, Dorothy. In our own
special ways.

P A ANNOUNCEMENT: Would all associates meet at
their spots for a good morning check-in?

TAMMY: *(Offstage)* If this is another hug session, I ain't
doing it!

*(*JANE *exits into the backroom again)*

WILMA: Come on back, hon.

TAMMY: 'Less they get us flu shots!

WILMA: Come on. Don't give up!

*(*WILMA *goes after* JANE. *End of scene)*

Scene Twenty-Five

(Outside the auditorium. TJ *is pacing, revved up from her
speech.* LYDIA *and* CHAI *join her).*

TJ: Where's that check? I'm supposed to get paid for
this!

*(*LYDIA *hands her an envelope,* TJ *tears it open.)*

TJ: We'll have to look for one of those check-cashing places.

LYDIA: Chai and I have something to tell you.

CHAI: We were quite hurt at first about the crickets up our...vaginas remark. But now we see that you are right. We allowed symbolization—

LYDIA: —infantilization!

CHAI: —of an idea to mask the real issues. And we are heartily sorry.

MAVIS: *(Entering. Pushing* TJ *to emphasize the she means business)* Who are you?!! You tell me right now!!! Who are you??

TJ: Whoa, lady!

CHAI: What are you doing to her?

MAVIS: At first I thought, "Clever presentation. And then, bad joke. And then poor woman. She's obviously brain damaged or something and I need to cover for her, so she won't be humiliated."
And then I'm the one who is humiliated!! I don't know who you are but you are not Jane Cavett or anyone who writes for academic publications. And here I am out there, in front of all my students and several of my colleagues, trying to go in all directions like some Chihuahua on linoleum. "Oh, you must mean this, or you must mean that," flinging jargon around to cover my ass 'cause you are waving your fraudulent ass for everyone to see.

LYDIA: Are you saying that she's not Jane Cavett?

MAVIS: I've never met Jane Cavett, but this woman is a fake and an imposter.

(MAVIS grabs the check out of TJ's *hand and tears it up.)*

TJ: What are you doing, you crazy bitch!

MAVIS: I want her out of my sight.

CHAI: Jane, what is she talking about?

TJ: Oh, whatever.

LYDIA: And what's that about you being assaulted?

MAVIS: Jane Cavett was assaulted by a student.
(To TJ) And here I thought you were so brave coming
out and speaking so soon after your injury.

LYDIA: I'm so sorry, Professor Pratt—

MAVIS: It's all right, dear. You just drove the car. And
your obviously Lesbian African-American friend
named after a drink you can get at Starbuck's is
besotted with—whoever this is. *(She exits.)*

LYDIA: You're not Jane Cavett?

TJ: Ummm, let me think. No.

LYDIA: You lied to us!

CHAI: Oh my god—who are you?

TJ: Someone you're in love with.

LYDIA: You deceived us!

TJ: Stop being such a couple of pussies. You decided
I was Jane Cavett. You HELPED ME be her. And you
know what? I like it. I fucking love it to death. I like
these clothes, too. I have legs and they look damn
good.

CHAI: You used me! You broke my heart!!

TJ: Wow! I am strong, I am the SuperCUNT!!

LYDIA: You disillusioned me!

TJ: That's good. You should write me a thank you note
on that pretty paper you can get in the drug store. I
figured out that "dis" on the front of a word means
'not" so I just gave you a dose of "NOT illusion" and
that's good.

LYDIA: I can't believe it. I can't believe another woman has treated me this way!

TJ: That's what equal rights is all about, baby. We can fuck over whoever we want to fuck over.

CHAI: I—I could kill you right now!! You deserve to die!

TJ: No. I CAN'T die now. You know why? I'll tell you. Me—this girl here got up in front of a whole room of those educated twats and spoke and they paid me one thousand dollars cash money.

LYDIA: They got mad at you!

TJ: Sure they got mad but that's conversation. We were conversing! And you know what—
(*To* CHAI)
Stop crying, Jesus!
—They listened to me. Cunts who wouldn't have given me the time of day.
THEY FUCKING THOUGHT I WAS SMART!!!

LYDIA: They thought you were dangerous.

TJ: Yeah…that, too. I gotta figure out how to com-bine the two. Because I figured it out. I'm NOT DUMB. I'm IGNORANT!!! Hey, why didn't you tell me I was ignorant!! You're supposed to be my friend and everything.

CHAI: It never occurred to me.

TJ: Oh, come on!! Why didn't you ever say, "Hey, TJ, you're ignorant!"

LYDIA: Because, first of all, we never knew your real name!

CHAI: Because we thought you were Jane Cavett! And she's not ignorant!

LYDIA: And, TJ, don't get madder than you already are, but you do NOT take criticism well.

TJ: Fuck you!! I do, too!! But it doesn't matter because I am HAPPY! I AM FUCKING HAPPY!!

LYDIA: You don't sound happy.

TJ: Well, I AM and nobody better fuck with this feeling or I will fucking KILL THEM!!

LYDIA: You. Get out. Of our lives.

CHAI: Yes, get out. GET OUT!!! GET OUT!!! GET OUT!!!! GET OUT!!!!

TJ: Whoa. Okay.

LYDIA: Don't come near me. Or her.

TJ: What about my stuff? I want all my cool stuff!!

LYDIA: We'll leave it on the porch

CHAI: Don't knock on the door.

TJ: Or what?

CHAI: I'LL CALL THE FUCKING POLICE ON YOU YOU FUCKING PIECE OF SHIT!!!

TJ: (*About* CHAI's *foul language*) Now there. There you sounded like a REAL person!! You can thank me for that!! Oh, you want me to leave you alone. You pussies. The fucking world is run by pussies!! For other pussies!!

(*End of scene*)

Scene Twenty-Six

(MOTHER *sits in her wheelchair with* MARTA, *a pleasant home medical aid.* MARTA *has some objects on her lap*)

MOTHER: I don't understand why you're here.

MARTA: Social Services sent me.

MOTHER: Social Services? We're not ready to receive guests. We need a better house for that.

MARTA: Because your household needs two incomes. And because your incontinence is preventing you from being a valuable member of the workforce.

MOTHER: Incontinence? I'm not sure I know what that means.

MARTA: Mrs Cavett, I believe you understand what I'm saying. Your case worker feels that you need some help accepting your situation and then moving on into the future

MOTHER: My situation? That I'm living in a slum surrounded by colored people?

MARTA: Your neighbors aren't "colored people." They are largely from Indonesia and Puerto Rico.

MOTHER: And what's this about "moving on into the future"? If I could move, I would move. If my daughter made enough money to allow us to move, I would move out of here in a second! And tell me this, why do you speak American English nearly perfectly and then suddenly put on an accent when you say words in Spanish?

MARTA: I am one-fourth Cuban. Marta is a Cuban name.

MOTHER: That's not enough to have a Spanish accent. My daughter speaks Spanish, but she says "porto rico" like the rest of us. Do you speak Spanish?

MARTA: No.

MOTHER: And my neighbors *are* colored. If I'm white, they are colored.

When I look at my skin, I see light peach. And that is the color of paint you would buy if you went to the paint store and wanted to paint a room "flesh-toned."

MARTA: All right, Mrs Cavett,

MOTHER: Don't patronize me. If you disagree, say so.

MARTA: I know you are operating out of your fear right now and trying to push me away, but I'm not leaving, Mrs Cavett. I'm here to talk about your gynecological exam.

MOTHER: I have cancer.

MARTA: No. No, you don't.

MOTHER: What are you doing with my medical records???

MARTA: The free clinic had the report faxed to our office. My speciality is in-home medical—

MOTHER: Your fax machine knows I have female trouble?

MARTA: Incontinence. And the fax machine doesn't care—it's seen worse. Oh, alright, since we are dealing with such personal matters as urine leakage, we should be completely honest with you, as a matter of trust. Your daughter asked us to visit you to talk to you about your leakage because it keeps you house-bound.

MOTHER: My daughter asked you to come and talk to me like this?

MARTA: Now. What has happened is that the pelvic floor—

MOTHER: (*Becoming more alarmed*) What floor!!? Where!!?

MARTA: Inside you.

MOTHER: I am sure I have no such thing.

MARTA: Yes, you do and it has weakened and your bladder has prolapsed—that means it has fallen a bit. Because of this, you have leakage issues.
(*Beat*)

But the good news is—there is treatment.
What you need to do is contract the vagina and release
it several times a day, You can do this anywhere and
that is the beauty of it.
So, let's try one.
Are you ready?
Contract. Hold. Release.
And another one.
Contract. Hold. Release.
Now you need to do several sets of these a day. For the
rest of your life, This will build up your pelvic floor.

MOTHER: I need to be alone now. I'm tired.

MARTA: You need to build up your pelvic floor.

Now let's do some calesthenics. I'll do them, too. I do
them every day, several times a day.

MOTHER: While you've been in my house??

MARTA: They're a habit.

MOTHER: While we've been talking??

MARTA: Look, I think you may need a little helper with
this.
*(She reaches inside her purse and pulls out a small, long box.
She takes the lid off and produces a phallic-like object and
sets it in front of MOTHER)*
Now, this is a Kegel exerciser. It opens up. Here. And
you put two springs in it—there are different sizes
to make exerciser bigger for more advanced muscle
building. Now what you do is lie flat as if you're
having a gynecological exam, on your bed, and insert
the exerciser into the vagina. Then Contract. Hold.
Release.
(She demonstrates by squeezing the exerciser inside her fist)
Contract. Hold. Release. You'll want to put some
lubricant on it before you insert it, of course. And

here's a condom for it. That's a little medical advisor
joke. It's good to have a joke about these things, you
know.

Now this one is for you. Use it, get used to it, make it a
part of your daily life and everything will improve.

Do you have any questions?

I'll leave you all of this. And these contact numbers—I
circled my name.

Oh, and you want to keep the Kegel exerciser clean.
So you should wash it, but only with soap and warm
water. Don't use any cleansers because they do leave a
residue that you will be able to feel inside your vagina.
You don't want that. No, we don't want our vaginas to
be irritated.

*(Making a puppet vagina with her hand and talking through
it with some special puppet voice)*

"Don't irritate me. Keep that Kegel exerciser clean—"

MOTHER: That's enough.

MARTA: *(As puppet vagina)* "—before you put it in me."
(Picks Kegel phallus up and makes it talk)
(As Kegel phallus)
"I'm going to make you stronger, Virginia"
(Puppet vagina voice)
"How did you know my name? Are you trying to
manipulate me?"
(Kegel phallus voice)
"All vaginas are named Virginia."

MOTHER: You may go.

MARTA: Mrs Cavett, you have to have a sense of humor
about these things—

MOTHER: Don't tell me what I have to have, young
woman of obviously foreign birth, and what good is a
sense of humor that you "Have to Have?"

MARTA: I was born in Chicago. And I'm leaving.

(MOTHER, *to the exiting* MARTA)

MOTHER: And the "thing" I'm supposed to have a
sense of humor about is
MY THING!!! And now listen to me! I'm sounding as
vulgar as this vulgar world!!
(She clears her lap of everything MARTA *has put there—the
Kegel phallus, the paper work, then tries to wheel off, can't.
In her rage, she stands up)*
Oh great. I can walk now. Even God has turned on me.
(She exits, walking in a halting manner, but walking.)

(End of scene)

Scene Twenty-Seven

(Pawn Shop. JO-JO *of* JO-JO'S WOMAN HELPING
WOMYN TWENTY-FOUR/SEVEN BARTER CENTER
is going over a list with TJ. TJ *is dressed well and is more
comfortable in the new persona and costume.)*

JO-JO: So, damn, you've cleaned house alright. This is a
lot of stuff you got here—enough for three people.

TJ: I'm, like, divesting myself of the empty objects of
this patriarchical market economy.

JO-JO: Do you have anything left?

TJ: Hell, yeah. Me.

JO-JO: That's it. Isn't it. That's all that matters.

TJ: I'd like cash.

JO-JO: No banks, either.

TJ: And one more thing. I know you do fake IDs.

JO-JO: Wait a minute. I dunno…

TJ: See, Jo-Jo, May I call you that? I really want to start
over. I'm turning my will and my life over to the Great

Goddess. And that includes my name. I want a new name.

JO-JO: I do these I Ds for women who are abused and need to escape their abuser.

TJ: Well, what if the abuser is the male hegemony. What if the abuser is the fucking phallocentric entire world?

JO-JO: It's important what you just said. I never know what those words mean exactly but when someone is throwing them around, I know—number one, they're smarter than me, and, number two, what they're saying is important. But I still don't know about this fake I D thing.

TJ: I thought I'd let you pick my new name. It's all about identity and its fucking fluidity.

JO-JO: Alright. Alright, then.
Lynda Carter.

TJ: Cool name. But I like the name Alice. Could we get that in there, somewhere?

(JO-JO *writes it down*)

JO-JO: Lynda Alice Carter.
(Going back into her work area)
I'll have this for you in a minute.
(Offstage)
Where you going next?

TJ: I don't know. I'll let the G G guide me. I'm sure She has something awesome in store for me.

(End of scene)

Scene Twenty-Eight

(JANE's apartment. JANE and WILMA enter. They are carrying fast food.)

JANE: Mo-ther? Some one's here.
(*To* WILMA)
Probibally—prabil—PROBABLY—a—a—sle—
SLEEPING. One bedroom her.Me. Here. Thanks ride.
Cold.

WILMA: Look, precious, you should just write this all
down because your speech is driving me crazy.
(*She sees the memo board and magic marker*)
Oh. So I'm not the only one who can't stand to hear
you talk. I mean, I know you're doing your best, I
know that.

(WILMA *hands* JANE *the memo board and marker.*)

WILMA: Okay. So how much do you—you got me
talking like you. Okay, how much do you pay for this
place?

(JANE *writes it.*)

WILMA: Yeah. You need another job—get a graveyard
shift!

(JANE *writes something else*)

WILMA: **Including** *utilities.* Well, your mother is going
to have to do something. Doesn't she have any skills?
How old a woman is she?

(JANE *writes.*)

WILMA: Seventy Two?

(JANE *writes.*)

WILMA: More like a hundred.

JANE: (*Spoken*) An old hundred.

WILMA: You get some disability?

JANE: For me?

WILMA: I meant for your mother, sugar. But now that
you mention it, I was wondering if you was deaf or
something like that. And had to learn to talk later.

JANE: No. Head injury. Don't remember.

(WILMA *points to the memo board and* JANE *starts writing again*)

WILMA: *(Reading what* JANE *writes)* You were robbed?
Took your car!
A woman?
A rich little bitch.

JANE: *(Speaks)* Yes.

WILMA: *(Reading as* JANE *writes with intensity)*
She got a good lawyer got time served plus two years
but that's only because I lived.

JANE: I wish I had died.

WILMA: Oh honey, don't say that.
Look, life is worth living. It really is. Honey. Believe
me. It is. Do you believe me?

(JANE *shakes her head no.)*

WILMA: You're just feeling this way because of
your blood sugar. Now, listen to me. Blood sugar is
everything. You gotta watch it. It will take you out.
I'm not kidding. You'll be halfway down the front of
some building you jumped off of and you'll remember,
"Shit! Crap! I'm not really suicidal, it's my damn blood
sugar!" That's why you need to eat.

(WILMA *opens the fast food and gives* JANE *a cheeseburger.*
JANE *tucks into it with enthusiasm)*
All this food—

JANE: *(Mouth full)* Two dollars!!

WILMA: See? Didn't I tell you?
The double cheeseburger—that's a dollar. Then,
instead of the pop, Coke, whatever, you get the ice
cream cone—it's cheaper and has more bulk. How can
you get meat, real meat—not bologna, not hot dogs—
and cheese and bread for a dollar? Cooked already?

If you bought them separately, they be a lot more
and then, if you're like me, where you gonna cook
anything? Hey, it's time. You need to go to bed.

JANE: Wilma? Stay.

WILMA: No, sugar. I got to get home.

JANE: Where?

WILMA: I live in my car. Hey, a lot of people do. It's
the cheapest housing you can get. All you pay is car
insurance and gas and a license and inspection every
year.

JANE: a lot of…money.

WILMA: About a hundred and sixty dollars a month.
Can't get an apartment for that. I'm saving up for an
apartment but I need two months rent to get one. There
are some cute ones right off seventy-five, there at the
interstate. I priced them—six-fifty a month. So that
would be I would need thirteen hundred dollars to get
one of them. But I'm saving. Got a couple of parking
tickets I had to pay. Stupid. I move the car all over the
city so the police don't get a bead on me because once
they do, they'll make it their business to hassle you,
like you're a public nuisance. So I got to be careful.
And I usually am. I've been living like this for two and
half years—that's two winters. But what I do then is I
go ahead and pay to get into one of these garages, like
under the mall. And I stay there for the worst nights.
It's worth it. And when it's all too much, I get a motel
room out on the old highway. They're desperate for
customers so I can get a room for fifty-dollars a night
at the old Budgetel. Take a long, long bath, watch
T V. It's heaven. I got six hundred dollars saved so by
next September, a year from now, I can move into an
apartment, I hope.

JANE: You could—

WILMA: Nuh-uh. Nope. Nice of you and everything, but I've got my spot picked out and I need to get going. Besides, I'm dying for a cigarette. I know they're expensive, but, dammit, I got a right to some pleasure in this life.

JANE: Smoke here.

WILMA: Baby, you're real sweet. But I'm not gonna stink up your nice apartment.

JANE: Please.

WILMA: I'm going to get a ticket.
(She crosses to comfort JANE.)
This is how they get us. We can't be mean like them. We can't be heartless like them. So we take care of each other. And so everybody has a little less. And we never get out of the hole.

(Lights fade on WILMA lighting up her cigarette and JANE leaning against her)

Scene Twenty-Nine

(MEGA-MART. MOTHER is wearing a red vest that looks more like a cloth sandwich board. It says, "ASSOCIATE". She speaks to various people coming in)

MOTHER: Welcome to Mega-Mart.
Welcome to Mega-Mart, sir. Oh sorry, Ma'am
Welcome to Mega-Mart…Ma'am?
Welcome to Mega-Mart. Whose little lovely child are you? Stay away little girl.
Welcome to Mega-Mart. Ho lah!
Welcome to Mega-Mart. Kah nee chee wah. Oh, you're not of foreign birth. I'm sorry. You orientals are so attractive, I was distracted.
Tammy? Tammy? I'm about two hours past by break time. Tammy? I've been standing for over four hours—

welcome to mega-mart—and, by the way, I wasn't
paid for the overtime. My hours didn't match up with
my records. There must be some mistake. Welcome
to Mega-Mart. I know I'm talking loud in front of
customers but I can never find management when I
need to speak about these things.
Welcome to whatever.
Tammy? I'm afraid if things don't get better here for
me and for my fellow employees, I'm going to form—
I've never done it before but I've seen it in movies—I'm
going to form a union.

*(Suddenly, there is the deafening sound of helicopters
circling overhead.)*

VOICEOVER: Would Associate Mrs Foster Cavett please
come to Room 101 for a sharing and caring session?

MOTHER: I made them use my full name. Where is
Room 101?

EDNA: *(Offstage)* The loading dock.

MOTHER: Oh, They want me to look at a new shipment
of lamps. I know a lot about lamps. I had some very
nice ones.

*(A female MEGA-MART corporate EXECUTIVE, enters,
wearing a power suit and sunglasses)*

EXECUTIVE: Come with me.

(MOTHER follows the EXECUTIVE off)

MOTHER: I hope there are no more of those hideous
monstrosities in floral shapes. They don't look like
lamps. People are confused—is it a lamp or a planter?
Slow down. Miss? Miss? I just got out of wheelchair!
Miss!

(End of scene)

Scene Thirty

(The offices of an editor, MIMI MANNING. *She answers the phone)*

MIMI: This is Mimi.

Aminda!! I can't be with you all day!! You're going to have to take some responsibility for your life and your actions!! I mean, if you want to kill yourself, I can't stop you!! I paid for Vassar and you flunked out. I paid for Bard and had to pull strings to get you into there and you flunked out. Do you know how hard it is to flunk out of Bard once you've been accepted? They try everything to graduate their students—that's the unwritten agreement they make with the parents. Pay a huge tuition and we guarantee that your child will graduate if it takes the entire faculty and a semi-tractor-trailer full of meds to do it!! But you still managed to flunk out. I'm at the end of my rope!!

(TJ enters.)

*(*MIMI *pretends she's talking to her cleaning woman instead of her fucked-up daughter)*
Yes, Zeenya. Finish the floors and then you can go home. Das vedanya.
(She hangs up the phone.)
Jane Cavett.
So this is what you look like.

TJ: Yeah.

MIMI: You've bounced back from your accident—what was it?

TJ: I was assaulted. By some crazy bitch who wanted my car.

MIMI: I can't imagine what it must have been like.

TJ: Yeah. It was some kind of hell alright.

MIMI: Did it, and I know this must be a tender topic, affect your speech?

TJ: Uhh—yeah. My words aren't as refined as they should be and I have trouble controlling my emotions.

MIMI: Well, I don't want to agitate you, but your manuscript is unsaleable. Liz sent it over after she finally received it and couldn't bring herself to tell you that. It's clearly about the loss of a civilization rather than having anything to do with post-modern feminist politics. And no one wants to read another book about the Mayans!

TJ: What the fuck? But I'm a teacher at a college and I'm supposed to be this undiscovered genius.

MIMI: Who told you that?

TJ: You mean I did all this work and you're telling me that it won't sell?

MIMI: That's right. It's not saleable. Yes. And I'm glad we got it out in the open and now I can tell Liz I saw you. Good. Fine. Excellent. So work on something I can sell and get back to me or to one of my assistants when you've finished it. So you can go. And I'll see you—. The elevator is… Are you alright?

TJ: So this is the world I'm in now—the world where people ask each other if they're alright. And everybody is because they have their basic needs met. But they still say they're alright, which they are, in these pitiful tones so we're supposed to think how noble they are to say they're alright when we think, because they want us to, that deep, deep, deep down inside they are hurt and lonely and sad and nobody understands them. No one knows their inner pain. "Oh, but I'd love to give you two hundred dollars towards your rent but you see, I'm too sad right now. I'm on my way to therapy or I have just left therapy and my inner child needs

comforting so I'm going to go buy it a brand new boat
and a lifetime supply of Odwalla Healthy Smoothies
and those new earphones that cut off all the sounds of
the world except my own heart which is bleeding for
you and all the poor poor poor pure poor living in the
garbage heaps with their noses stuck in gluebags like
skinny ponies by the way could I get a pony for my
child's birthday party only I want a chubby pony that
reminds me to send two hundred dollars to the Save
Animals Fund."

MIMI: Are you aware of how angry you are right now?
Shouldn't you take your meds or do your breathing—
whatever you've developed to control your anger?
Because head injuries can change people in significant
ways.

TJ: Tell me something I don't know. Oh, and that tone
you just used on me? That sounds like I just barfed or
farted a big long one.

MIMI: What I'm saying is that these things you've been
saying to me? In your agitated state? They should be
in the book. It's much more alive then that arcane,
pretentious crap that's in here now. People want to
read things they can understand.

TJ: Just tell me what people want and I'll give it to
them! All my life I've been trying to find something I
can do that people will pay for—and pay good money
for—not shit money for cleaning toilets and doing
people's laundry and waiting on their drunken asses
in all-night diners or selling them piles of crappy snack
food in the mini-mart and smiling. No, something that
I can sell that they will buy for decent money. Money
to live on. Money to keep from taking everybody's
shit. Money to sleep on and when you wake up it's still
there. That kind of money!

MIMI: And that's what I can sell—your voice, your
real voice. I say, dump the Mayans—they're gone and
you were only using them as a paradigm for Islam
and everyone will know it. What I can sell is life and
truth. But for the popular market. Wise-cracking anti-
establishment, balloon-popping, irreverent humor I can
sell. When things are bad, people need to laugh more.
That's why oppressed minorities have the best humor.
I mean, who's funnier that the Irish or the Jews or the
Blacks…black people? Oppression equals HUMOR.
Armenians! I mean, who's funnier that the Armenians?

TJ: But I'm not funny. I AM NOT FUCKING FUNNY!!

(MIMI laughs a lot at this.)

MIMI: Sorry. But you are. Sometimes the thing we're
best at is so close to us that we can't see it.

TJ: Okay. Okay. Well, let's just clear everything away,
huh? I want to use my real name now. I'm not Jane
Cavett. I am Lynda Alice Carter—Lynda with a "y."
Read my I D.

MIMI: But you said you were Jane Cavett.

TJ: News flash. I never was. I just used poor Jane's
misfortune for my own benefit. Because you wouldn't
have seen me if I hadn't. Fact is, I'm from Jane's
community and I haven't been able to stomach the
crap she's been handing out. I know I got things to say,
important things, but I could never get anywhere with
any of my ideas.

MIMI: Where are you staying?

TJ: Hotel.

MIMI: Where?

TJ: Over there by the…thing.

(Long beat. MIMI looks at TJ.)

MIMI: You're going to move in with my daughter. It's a nice place with no pets but there are plants that have to be watered. And there's a computer. I need someone to watch her. She's trying to get off oxycontin and who knows what else.

TJ: Sounds…okay, I guess.

MIMI: Here. Here's four hundred and thirty-two dollars from my petty cash. You'll be getting an advance in a check from—

TJ: Just give it in cash money directly to me.

MIMI: You don't trust the patriarchy at all, do you?

TJ: Hegemically speaking, no one should trust anyone. Because the low want to bring the high ones down, mug them, really, and the high want to keep what they got so they don't want the low to even touch them with their failure cooties.

MIMI: Put that in your book!! That is pure gold! And keep my daughter clean! And all will be available to you.

TJ: I want that in writing.

MIMI: You're a lot smarter than people think you are, aren't you?

TJ: Fuck yeah. Absolutely. I mean fuck, yeah.

MIMI: I'll send the paperwork over to Aminda's apartment—that's my daughter's name. I'll get a car to take you to your…hotel…and then to my daughter's apartment. It's a two-bedroom in Turtle Bay.

TJ: That's great. I'd love to get out of this city.

MIMI: Ah, good. Just take the elevator down to the garage. So we have a deal?

(They shake hands and TJ *exits.* MIMI *gets on phone.)*

MIMI: Ahmed?

Oh, okay. Carlos.

Woman on her way down. Very sketchy. But she'll
do as a babysitter until I can find another rehab for
Aminda.

Take her where she needs to go and then to Aminda's.
She doesn't know shit about New York. But that's
good. She'll stay where we put her.

(*End of scene*)

Scene Thirty-One

(MOTHER *sits in the dark in the cheap chair from Linens &
Things. She is no longer wearing her* ASSOCIATE *apron.*
JANE *enters, carrying Chinese food take-out*)

JANE: You still sitting in the dark?

Mother, every—body gets fired sometimes. I been
fired—oh—three four times? We'll be alright. I'm
working that shift at Cumby. And I'm feeling better
better. And you are, too? Mother. Look! Both of us
walking on our own.

MOTHER: What is that horrible smell?

JANE: Moo-shoo pork. And chick—en fried rice. Two
fortune cookies.

MOTHER: We're eating take-out prepared by
immigrants.

JANE: Pedro and his fam—ily have been here for
gener—ations, Mother.

MOTHER: I am hungry.

JANE: Shall we op—en our fortune cookies—first?

MOTHER: Oh god! No fortunes. Let's just eat.

(*End of scene*)

Scene Thirty-Two

(In Mimi's *daughter's [*Aminda*] apartment. TJ is trying to work on the computer but it's getting the best of her)*

TJ: Fuck! Stop! Stop doing that!!

*(*Aminda *walks over to the computer and pushes a button, walks away.)*

TJ: What did you do?

Aminda: *(Groggy)* Num lock. Pushed it.

TJ: Okay, I got it. Thanks.

Aminda: Yo. *(She exits)*

TJ: Fuck

(At computer, something else is out of control. Aminda *strolls in, pushes a button problem solved.)*

TJ: What that time?

Aminda: Cap lock. Don't lock. Wanna get high? I'm high.

TJ: What the fuck?! You're supposed to be getting clean. You're gonna make me look bad. I'll lose this place to stay. What did you take?

Aminda: Some…thin.

TJ: Well, we're gonna find out!

(TJ grabs Aminda *and puts her fingers down her throat, making her gag. They exit in this position. Sound of barfing offstage. Then more barfing. Then more barfing. Then a flush. Then the sound of a shower running and* Aminda *yelling from offstage)*

Aminda: It's cold!! Dammit!! What the hell? What are you—JESUS CHRIST WHAT THE FUCK!!! My mouth tastes GROSS!!

TJ: Turn around!

AMINDA: You turn around! Fuck you!

(TJ *re-enters room, finds a big roll of duct tape and exits into the bathroom again. Sounds of lots of swearing from* AMINDA, *then silence. A couple beats more and* TJ *and* AMINDA *re enter.* AMINDA *is wrapped up, swaddled, in a big towel that is taped around with duct tape. She looks a little like a mummy or a giant papoose and can barely walk.* TJ *is moving her along.* TJ *props* AMINDA *up and goes back to the computer)*

AMINDA: Is this necessary?

TJ: YES. I have work to do. Fall asleep and I'll slap you awake!

(Lights fade as TJ *stares at the computer screen.)*

Scene Thirty Two B—

(Lights come back up and TJ *is bleary-eyed at the computer. She shakes her head to wake up and then sees that* AMINDA *has fallen asleep)*

TJ: Oh Christ.

(TJ *goes over to* AMINDA *and lowers her in mummification on to the floor, slaps her awake and then rolls her around like a log until* AMINDA *is wide awake.)*

TJ: Can you hear me!!

*(*AMINDA *nods.)*

TJ: SAY SOMETHING!!

AMINDA: Peanut butter sandwich.

TJ: You're all right. I'm gonna get some writing done. I'm using pencil and paper. Fuck this computer. I'll get you some food later.

AMINDA: *(Lying on the floor)* That's alright, I'll just stand here.

TJ: Fuck!!!

(TJ *stands* AMINDA *up, leaning against something*)

AMINDA: Feels good to lie down.

TJ: If you die on me, I will fucking kill you!!!

AMINDA: I'm fine, yo.

(TJ *grabs all the coffee she can reach and starts feeding it to* AMINDA.)

TJ: You know what I was thinking while you were in there puking your guts out? I was thinking that Hegemony happens. That you can't keep it from happening. So the thing is to find the strings that all those whoever they are at the top of the Hegemony are, you know, pulling. And then to jerk those strings real hard and out of their hands or shimmy up one 'til you can get to the pulling end and then grasp that sucker tight in you hand and hold on and don't let anyone take that string away from you. I have been all my fucking life at the wrong end of the string!
And you know what, Aminda? Aminda?

AMINDA: Yo.

TJ: Say, yes, TJ, Jane, Lynda—what is my fucking name? Anyway, stop saying "yo" because you are not a rapper, okay? You are a young woman, or will be, if I have to stay up all night and walk you around until you're sober.

AMINDA: Okay.

TJ: Alright. Tune into me here. Eye contact. Eyes open. I am going to write this book, even if I have to carve it into your arm. Because you know what, you spoiled little twat? Poverty does not make you noble. When you have nothing, morality and ethics are luxuries. And that's why rich people make me mad when they don't use their morals or their ethics and do evil shit

just because they're, like, greedy. They don't ever have
to lie, steal and cheat to live, but they do it, anyway. I
want a good life. I don't want to be so fucking angry all
the fucking time!!!

AMINDA: Stop yelling aw-ight? I'm okay, aw-ight?
Make me a sandwich. Or I will.
I will. Okay, okay? You need to chill. Besides, my
mother isn't going to give you a fucking book. She's
going to take your sayings that you're so, like, full
of? And make them into one of those daily calendars
where you rip off the pages. Because you're, like,
a poor risk. Yo. And she knows you'll never finish
the book, never thought you'd finish it. And mainly
because my mother fucks everyone over. Yo. All you
are is a big babysitter for a big baby that's me. YO!

TJ: YOU ARE NOT HELPING ME WITH MY
ANGER!!!

AMINDA: I'm incapable of helping anyone. Haven't you
noticed? I'm a fucking drug addict!!

(TJ exits. AMINDA hops around}

AMINDA: Hey! Hey! Don't leave me!! Hey!!

(Door slams. TJ is gone)

(End of scene)

Scene Thirty-Three

(SUSAN, in prison, mopping again, but efficiently)

SUSAN: You forgot all about me, didn't you? Well,
turns out circumstantial evidence is enough if they're
fed up with the likes of young stupid white girls whose
mothers have given up on them, but that's in the past,
so just pay attention 'cause I'm going to tell you how
to make Jell-0 wine. You get a package of Jello from the

prison store, add some water and stir and you let it sit for weeks and finally it ferments and you drink it. And if you don't throw up, you can get a little buzz on. Now about sex. A lot of inmates have sex in here but you need to do it with the guards and on the down low—that's authentic Black talk I learned from my roommate—the one before last. Because any handholding or hugging or touching even is not allowed *among* us inmates. And sex is okay with the guards until it's found out and your special guard gets walked off the property, never to return. If you are a lesbian, then you are shit out of luck because the guards are male. I've decided to be celibate for health, safety, and self-respect reasons.

You can get drugs if you really have to have them. But you can't count on steady delivery so the best thing is to clean-up and stay clean. I do mopping and one of my jobs is cleaning up the dry-out tank. When someone is coming off drugs, they shit a lot of green liquid and can't always make it to the toilets. They tremble and gag a lot and want to die and say so but they're too weak to even jump out of a window or hang themselves with sheets, not that they could get away with that anyway with everybody watching. Most of the women in here have felonies related to drug use and selling and usually it's the boyfriend or husband who is doing the business and they get swept up in the raid, too, and they're usually stoned because they are users so they're too out of it to get away. And they wouldn't leave without their children. And then the children, well, they'll be here someday probably.

I'll tell you something. What I miss most is just privacy. The only way I can have it is to pull the covers over my head. And it's a relief. To do that.. Because all we have is the television and that is enough to make you want to puke. All these voices of people who are acting so all you hear is this hyped up talk and shreds of music and recorded laughter, There's nothing stupider than watching a bunch of depressed women staring at a sit com with a laugh track. They're like these huge, sad gods staring at the little box full of tiny people having great lives.

Being in here has made me a better person. And that's what I'm going to tell the parole officers. This was meant to be because there are no accidents so it's part of God's plan for me.

Oh yeah, and I've been born again and accepted Jesus Christ as my personal savior.

It was something to do.

(She reaches into her pocket and pulls out a small tape recorder and speaks right into the mic)

So that's it for now, Mom. Call me sometime.

(She turns the tape recorder off and exits cleanly because this time she didn't mop herself into a corner)

(End of scene)

Scene Thirty-Four

(A year later. A bus stop with one of those clear plastic shelters. JANE waits. She's dressed pretty much like TJ was at the beginning of the play. A female bus DRIVER enters, waits. Gradually more people enter, wait. No one should have an umbrella or a raincoat and the sudden storm that happens further in the scenes should catch them all by surprise)

DRIVER: Oh man. I'm going to be late for work.

WOMAN 1: You drive these buses? That's funny.

DRIVER: It's not my route. Don't blame me. They don't have enough drivers but they won't hire more. Stingy motherfuckers.

WOMAN 2: This is the 23A, isn't it?

WOMAN 1: The bus that never comes.

WOMAN 2: Whose decision was it to put a shelter here and not over there, too?

DRIVER: Don't look at me. "Hegemony happens", y'all.

WOMAN 2: You got that calendar, too?

WOMAN 1: "The low want to mug the high ones, and the high want to keep what they got."

DRIVER: "All you unemployed, don't touch me with your failure cooties".

(TJ enters. She's dressed in a uniform from some hourly-wage business, and looks a bit more "girly" and cleaned-up than at the beginning of the play)

DRIVER: I don't know about the rest of you, but I'm walking over to 4th to get the 110.

WOMAN 2: I'll go, too. I can't be late for work.

(They leave.)

WOMAN 1: But there's no shelter there. *(Looks at her watch)* Damn.

(They all exit, leaving JANE and TJ.)

(Sound of thunder in the distance)

JANE: They will get wet.

TJ: *(About her work uniform)* I knew I shouldn't wear this thing. I thought I was saving time.

(JANE and TJ look at each other, then look away.)

TJ: Maybe I can make a run for it.

JANE: You're gonna need a raincoat.

(TJ and JANE turn their heads to look again. Lights down as they stand, locked in each other's gaze)

END OF PLAY

www.ingramcontent.com/pod-product-compliance
Lightning Source LLC
Chambersburg PA
CBHW070023110426
42741CB00034B/2352